MW00998826

Praise for

COOK. HEAL. GO VEGAN!

"Chef Bai's delicious, colorful dishes will make you look at plants in a new way. This book is perfect for the novice chef who wants to incorporate more veggie-rich meals in their diet and the more experienced health-conscious eater alike."

—**Liz Moody,**
BESTSELLING AUTHOR OF *Healthier Together*

"More than just a cook-book, this is a guide to nourishing your body, your soul, the people around, the animals, and the planet. It will be a game changer for anyone wanting to eat more plants!"

—**Tigerlily (Dara Hayes),**
DJ, PRODUCER, AND VEGAN ACTIVIST

"Chef Bai truly talks the talk and walks the plant-powered walk. Her story of healing is inspiring, and I want to make every recipe in this book!"

—**Jessica Murnane,**
AUTHOR OF *One Part Plant* AND *Know Your Endo*

"Chef Bai has intertwined her culinary skills and plant-based lifestyle so beautifully in *Cook. Heal. Go Vegan!* Her recipes are always bright, colorful, and full of flavor, proving that you don't have to give up your favorites on a vegan diet!"

—**Hannah Sunderani,**
AUTHOR AND FOUNDER OF TWO SPOONS

BREAKING UP WITH DAIRY

Also by
Bailey Ruskus:
COOK.
HEAL.
GO VEGAN!
A Delicious Guide to
Plant-Based Cooking
for Better Health
and a Better World
ANTI DAIRY VIBE CLUB

BREAKING UP WITH DAIRY

100 Indulgent Plant-based Recipes for Cheese (and Butter, Cream, and Milk) Lovers Everywhere

Bailey Ruskus

CHEF BAI * **Photography by Steve and Bailey Ruskus**

FOREWORD BY CARLEIGH BODRUG,
New York Times bestselling author of *PlantYou* and *PlantYou: Scrappy Cooking*

NEW YORK BOSTON

NOTE: The information in this book is true and complete to the best of our knowledge. This book is intended only as an informative guide for those wishing to know more about health issues. In no way is this book intended to replace, countermand, or conflict with the advice given to you by your own physician. The ultimate decision concerning care should be made between you and your doctor. We strongly recommend you follow their advice. Information in this book is general and is offered with no guarantees on the part of the authors or Balance. The authors and publisher disclaim all liability in connection with the use of this book.

Cover design by Terri Sirma
Cover photographs by Steve Ruskus

Balance
Hachette Book Group
1290 Avenue of the Americas
New York, NY 10104
@GCPBalance

First Edition: February 2025

Balance is an imprint of Grand Central Publishing. The Balance name and logo are registered trademarks of Hachette Book Group, Inc.

The publisher is not responsible for websites (or their content) that are not owned by the publisher.

The Hachette Speakers Bureau provides a wide range of authors for speaking events. To find out more, go to hachettespeakersbureau.com or email HachetteSpeakers@hbgusa.com.

Balance books may be purchased in bulk for business, educational, or promotional use. For information, please contact your local bookseller or Hachette Book Group Special Markets Department at special.markets@hbgusa.com.

Print book interior design
by Toni Tajima.

Library of Congress Cataloging-in-Publication Data has been applied for.

ISBNs: 978-0-306-83352-6 (paper over board),
978-0-306-83353-3 (ebook)

Printed in China

APS

10 9 8 7 6 5 4 3 2 1

This book is for the voiceless.
For the mamas and their babies.
Because it's important to remember that
cows don't make milk because they're cows,
they make milk because they're mothers.

Contents

5. Get Sauced

6. Main Meals Worthy of a Third Date

7. Life of the Party

8. The Sweetest Thing

Foreword

Hey, Friend,

So you've found yourself in the throes of a breakup with dairy, huh? Welcome to the club! If you're anything like me, you've probably had some melodramatic moments staring longingly at a wedge of Brie, wondering if life could ever be the same without it. Spoiler alert: it can, and it's about to get a whole lot cheesier—in the best way possible.

Enter Chef Bailey Ruskus, our dairy-free fairy godmother armed with recipes so divine, you'll swear she's performing plant-based wizardry. Forget about the dairy dilemma because Bailey holds the key to all your creamy, melty, cheesy dreams—without the stomachache.

Think plant-based cheese that actually melts (yes, miracles do happen), truffle fries that'll make your taste buds do a happy dance, and tiramisu espresso so decadent, you'll swear it's straight from the streets of Italy. And that's just the tip of the oat milk iceberg . . . Hungry yet? I know I am!

I want you to consider this cookbook your culinary therapist, guiding you through the stages of grief (yes, cheese withdrawal is a thing) and helping you emerge on the other side as a proud member of the anti-dairy vibe club.

But this isn't just about food—it's about the journey. I always say going plant-based was one of the single best decisions I've made in my life. Like finally pulling the plug on a toxic ex, saying bye-bye to dairy left me feeling lighter, less bloated, and more inspired than ever in the kitchen.

Chef Bai's story takes this one step further. Classically trained at Le Cordon Bleu with years of restaurant and private cheffing experience, Bailey used the power of whole, plant-based foods to help her on the path to healing chronic pain and endometriosis. That dedication and tenacity to create a diet focused on abundance rather than restriction—one that feeds both the body and soul—is evident with every turning page.

So whether you're diving headfirst into the world of plant-based eating or just dipping your toe into the dairy-free fondue, this cookbook is your trusty sidekick on your breakup journey. Raise a glass of almond milk and get ready to say "cheese" (the plant-based kind, of course). Your taste buds will thank you, and so will the cows.

To new beginnings.

Carleigh Bodrug,
New York Times bestselling author
PlantYou and *PlantYou: Scrappy Cooking*

Introduction

What was the hardest breakup you ever went through? For me, most people would assume it was the guy who broke my heart when I was twenty-three, but in reality, the hardest breakup I ever went through was with the dairy industry.

I'm a professional chef of Polish descent who was trained at Le Cordon Bleu. I was also an American kid of the '90s, and dairy was a part of my identity and daily life. Regardless of whether it was creamy sauces, buttercream frosting, Muenster slices from the deli, or the best grilled cheese of my life made with Gruyère, dairy was always kind of my thing.

My battle with endometriosis made me take a hard look at everything in my life, and my relationship with dairy was at the top of my list. I was beginning to learn about the effects of excess estrogen in the body, and dairy products (especially the high-fat cheeses I loved so much) were the biggest culprit in my diet. Doctors and experts like Michael Klaper, Neal D. Barnard, T. Colin Campbell, and Michael Greger were key teachers for me during this time, and I even started a podcast so I could interview as many experts as possible, to figure out once and for all how all people with periods could begin to heal a different way.

I read books like *The Period Repair Manual*, *Know Your Endo*, *How Not to Die*, and *Your Body in Balance*. I became obsessed with finding a better way to live—I wanted a new lease on life, not just for myself but for other people like me as well.

I learned that my unshakable craving for cheese during my luteal phase was not only physically addicting but it equaled a really painful and unbearable period. I truly couldn't imagine a life without cheese, and it took many trips to the hospital, and a pretty gnarly surgery, for my boyfriend (now husband) to force me to really look at the toxic and codependent relationship I had with the dairy industry. The thing is, it wasn't just personal, it was professional, it was social, and it was all-encompassing in my life. To break up with dairy, I had to be okay with not fitting into the boys' club of chef culture. I had to change everything about the way I wined and dined with friends. And, most challenging of all, I had to learn the hard truths about how horrible the dairy industry actually is.

This book isn't about me, though. It's about you. It's about all of us. It's about the tight grip the dairy industry has on our school systems and how about 68 percent of the population is lactose intolerant. It's about the rising numbers in breast and prostate cancer. It's about government subsidies on dairy products in low-income communities of color with the highest rates of heart disease and type 2 diabetes. It's about the big animal agriculture industry and how it's the third leading cause of climate change. It's about the mama cows and mama goats who get used and abused and cry out for their babies. It's about capitalism, big business, and government lobbyists who will do anything to get dairy in everything. When you pull back the layer of why we're all addicted to cheese, you realize that it was designed this way. And dairy truly is the toxic, abusive, and narcissistic boyfriend you just can't get away from.

Yes, this is a book about dairy alternatives. But more than anything, this book is about our future. The future of food and the future of our personal and planetary health. We're taking off the rose-colored glasses and breaking up with dairy for good.

This book is really about finding our joy and how to rebuild our lives post-breakup. Breaking up with dairy isn't just a personal choice or a diet trend, *it's a movement*. The contents of this book will change the way you see things, and will smash your own expectations of what a dairy-free life looks like. I promised myself that the only way I would leave dairy behind was if I could have just as much pleasure in my life without it. I needed to create just-as-delicious food and blow my own mind with flavors and textures that never made me feel like I was missing out. The recipes in this book are the creamy and decadent vibes you'd get from classic recipes that are taken to the next level. They do all you need and more, without the downfall after that cheese high. It's a new relationship full of pleasure in a way that builds you up without ever bringing you down.

When I look back at that toxic relationship I had with my ex-boyfriend, I think to myself, *What the fuck was I actually thinking?!* Years from now, when we look back at our consumption of dairy and factory farming, we'll also be wondering what the fuck we were thinking.

This book is not only the catalyst for a dairy-free future; it's the blueprint. It's for us, and it's for the future generations that come after us. Regardless whether you were born in 1952 or 2002, it's not too late. It's a reminder that we all deserve better and the future of food starts with us.

A Note to the Dairy Farmers

At first glance, this book might seem like it's a rally against you, and honestly, in ways it is—against the systems you use. What I really hope is that we can all find a way to move forward with our food system with more compassion for animals and in a way that takes better care of our land. I know that dairy farmers specifically are facing their own challenges with low consumer demand, rising costs, lower industry prices, and higher regulations. To put it simply, I know it is a challenging time to be a farmer. I know I can speak for the younger generations when I say that our goal is not to just shut you down with our consumer choices, but hopefully to be a catalyst for change in what and how you farm. With plant-based-food demand rising, and overall the rally and pressure for climate action increasing, my hope with this movement is that we can work together to find change and better practices for agriculture, moving forward. We all still have a lot to learn, but what I do know is that we can get so much further and take better care of one another if we work together to make a better future for us all.

Axl, rescued goat from the dairy industry. He is now living his life of freedom away from harm at Sale Ranch Animal Sanctuary in Temecula, California.

1. The 5 STAGES of BREAKING UP

DAIRY IS EVERYWHERE, from your favorite coffeehouse to your local grocery store to your best friend's dinner party. It's in your favorite drinks, snacks, and desserts. Before we get into the delicious recipes, the five stages of breaking up are not only a necessary part of grief, but they also make up your *why*. This chapter is a reminder that your toxic ex may try to come back into your life, but it's the heavy dose of therapy and awareness that will keep you strong and moving forward on a path without them. It's knowing that you can't live in regret, but you can be happy that the breakup happened and know that, in the long run, you're better for it.

STAGE 1
Denial

Denial is a safe space, which is why we often want to stay in it forever. In denial, we get to continue with the habits that we're comfortable with. In denial, we don't ask for accountability, and in denial, we rarely act courageous.

To act courageously and to radically change our lives, we must open ourselves up to the truth and really understand and digest the reality of what's going on. To help us with this phase of the breakup, I interviewed Dr. Neal Barnard, founder of the Physicians Committee for Responsible Medicine. This committee has over eighteen thousand physicians as members who are working tirelessly with policymakers, politicians, the medical community, the media, and people like you and me, to create a better world for people and animals alike. Dr. Barnard mentioned these systems and influences that help shape our collective denial:

THE DAIRY CHECK-OFF PROGRAM
This is a federally mandated program that has a huge impact on how much milk and cheese people are consuming. Think: MyPlate, and advertisements like "Got Milk?" Dairy is subsidized, which simply means that financial grants funded by public tax money are given to private and corporate dairy farms and companies, to drive down production costs. Direct subsidies by the government influence the price of dairy products, making them more accessible and affordable, and making sure that the industry is getting paid.

LOBBYING AND MISINFORMATION
The dairy lobby influences against climate change legislation and spends an incredible amount of money to keep the misinformation alive through advertising and social media. The meat and dairy industry act together to block climate policy that would require them to limit production to meet emission and pollution limits and standards. These groups have spent over $200 million alone on lobbying against these climate-related issues.

ADDICTING THE MASSES
There are government advertising contracts with fast-food companies to make cheese more prominent on their menu. That triple-cheese bacon cheeseburger? It's a ploy to do one thing: sell more cheese. Milk advertisements are the only ads allowed in public schools. Cheese has been stashed in food assistance programs to get rid of it, for the dairy farmers to keep production so high.

MILK IS FOR BABIES
Humans and all other mammals have lactase enzymes to digest milk as infants, and those enzymes leave the body post-infancy. Simply put, milk is for babies, not adults.

LATE-STAGE CAPITALISM
We have the power to influence what happens next. We get to vote with our dollars. When enough people stop buying dairy, and enough milk gets wasted, things will inevitably change. We can use late-stage capitalism to our advantage, and your learning this now will help you move past denial and into the future of food for us all.

STAGE 2
Bargaining

When you're wondering if it's time to break up, you end up bargaining with yourself and everyone around you, to convince yourself that everything is fine. I can't even count the number of times I've heard my girlfriends talk about their toxic relationships and say, "But Bai, when it's good, it's so good!"

So, like any smart person would do, we're making a pros and cons list:

THE PROS:	THE CONS:	
I can't lie; it's obviously delicious.	A major polluter of local communities, air quality, and fresh water	Can cause acne and weight gain
High in protein	A leading cause of greenhouse gas emissions	Can trigger gut issues, such as colic, in infants
Easily accessible	Incredibly cruel and inhumane to animals	Dairy is the most common allergen among children.
High in nutrients, including calcium, magnesium, potassium, and vitamin D	Cheese is the largest source of saturated fat in the American diet.	Millions of gallons of milk get dumped every year.
Affordable	Can put you at a higher risk for lung, prostate, breast, and ovarian cancer	Inefficient use of fresh water
Part of cultural foods	Can put you at a higher risk for type 2 diabetes and heart disease	Inefficient use of land to grow grain to feed livestock
An easily accessible formula for infants	Can put you at a higher risk for bone fracture	May contain antibiotics
	Can be physically addicting	Can contain high amounts of estrogen
	Dairy, itself, does not build strong bones.	Sixty-eight percent of the global population has lactose malabsorption.

STAGE 3
Anger

This is one of the most productive stages of grief and breaking up because I truly think that this phase fuels the most action. It's easy to get angry at the lobbyists, the lawmakers, the CEOs, and everyone else who is perpetuating this cycle. And, I mean, why wouldn't we be pissed? Just revisit the Cons list. Add to that:

THE DAIRY INDUSTRY LOOKS AT COWS AS NOTHING MORE THAN A PRODUCT AND MILK MACHINE. It uses cruel practices, such as artificial insemination, taking babies from mother cows immediately after birth and then slaughtering them shortly after for veal, or using them to produce more milk as future dairy cows.
WHEN THE MAMA COW'S TIME IS UP, OR THEY COLLAPSE FROM EXHAUSTION, THEY, TOO, ARE SLAUGHTERED.

All this for what? A glass of milk? A grilled cheese? Is it all really worth it? I don't know about you, but for me, this amount of emotional baggage is a red flag no matter how much personal pleasure a relationship brings.

STAGE 4
Depression

Having a new level of awareness can be overwhelming, but it's important to remember that as humans, past infancy, we don't need dairy. Dairy does not have to be a part of our evolution; it's a cultural product, and the best part about that is that, at any time, we can be the charge of a new trend and a new way of doing things.

This also might be a good time to mention that coming off cheese can actually make you chemically depressed; that FOMO (fear of missing out) you're feeling, well, it's your body's way of letting you know you're actually addicted. Casomorphins, which are compounds that stimulate the same receptors in the brain that narcotics do, are why you're feeling this way. Originally, this is part of the mother-infant bond—you get protein, nutrients, and some delicious feel-good hormones. As a baby, it keeps you happy, nourished, and needing more from your mom. Of course, humans figured out how to keep this feel-good feeling long past infancy and capitalize on it. But this feel-good isn't meant for you; it's for the baby cows and goats and sheep. You are, in fact, not a baby cow, and that milk really isn't for you. If she's not your mama, it's not your milk. Sorry but . . . someone had to say it.

At this stage, you might be realizing that you need to move on, and although you know you'll be better for it, it takes some time to fully accept the reality of where you are. Just promise me you'll continue the breakup after this stage because it only gets better from here.

STAGE 5
Acceptance

So . . . now what? You're tapped in, tuned in, and a different part of you has been turned on. You realized that you needed to get out of it, so you broke up, and now you're ready to see what life looks like after the breakup—and that is where the rest of this book comes in.

Breaking up with dairy doesn't mean you'll never eat cheese again or have your favorite dessert; it just means you get to have it a different way, without all the baggage. What comes next is the beautiful experiment of life after a breakup. It's the version of you that exists outside your comfort zone. The version of you that exists outside excuses, drama, and heartbreak. It's the part of the breakup where you get to live life on your own terms, and it can look however you want it to. You can speed date and immediately make everything in this book, or you can dip one toe in, just go out on the weekends, and pick one or two recipes to meal prep.

This is the fun part. This is where you get to be the change, and it starts with you right in your own kitchen. You're now in the game for personal longevity, for going against the norm, and for better options for all.

2. Finding YOUR PERFECT MATCH

TO REBUILD YOUR LIFE POST-BREAKUP, we have to hit the reset button, so to speak. When we end relationships, we also *must* get rid of the things that remind us of our ex. We have to rid ourselves of the temptations to go back, and with some effort, we can begin to clearly see our life without them.

Out with the Old; in with the New

After every breakup, the key to moving on is sifting through our life and ridding evidence of the last relationship. I'm talking closets of clothes, separating photos to their own photo album, clearing out the dreaded social media photos, and blocking the "ex" from our socials to avoid the self-torturous "check-ins." Now, let's move this theme to your kitchen.

Before the restock begins, the purge is essential. Go through your cabinets, pantry, and fridge, and either finish, get rid of, or donate anything that has any of the following ingredients:

WHOLE AND NONFAT MILK	CONDENSED MILK
MILK FAT	CREAM
MILK POWDER	GHEE
WHEY	YOGURT
CASEIN	CHEESE
COLOSTRUM	BUTTER

Be sure to read through the ingredients of all packaged goods. You'd be surprised how many companies sneak in milk fat or milk powder to make processed foods like chips more addicting. You can do a huge overhaul and do this all at once, or take it one product at a time, one drawer at a time, one day at a time. It's up to you, boo—you do what works for you!

The Pantry Restock

Once the purge is complete, it's time to begin the restock. The important thing to note here is that you don't have to do this all at once, and the restock can simply begin at the start of the first recipe you want to create. Every new recipe you make, you get the chance to stock up on new ingredients. With that said, you can also view this section as a master list to refer back to.

The best way to do this restock is to look at buying in bulk. Buy online for specialty ingredients, look at grocery outlets and, of course, bulk shopper stores. Relying on your hometown grocer might leave you empty-handed, but if you do find what you need, you might be spending way more money than you need to. The goal is to make the switch budget-friendly and easy-breezy! Purchasing nuts, seeds, herbs, and oils can get pricey, so planning ahead will allow you to do this in the most cost-effective way while staying on budget. The best part? Most of these ingredients are shelf-stable pantry ingredients, so you don't need to worry about them going sour quickly.

Having a stocked pantry is key to really thriving on a dairy-free diet. Understanding why we use the ingredients we do can also help you create your own cheeses, milks, and sauces long past trying out every recipe in this book.

NUTS

Cashews: Cashews are every dairy-free person's dream for a replacement. They're fatty and so versatile, and create a rich and smooth texture in just about anything. This is why you see cashews in a lot of vegan or dairy-free recipes. Cashews are filled with a neurochemical called tryptophan, which turns into serotonin in our body. They are also rich in vitamin B_6 and magnesium. With this nutrient powerhouse, cashews can chemically make you happier, they'll help you live longer, and they are an excellent remedy for a broken heart.

Blanched Slivered Almonds: These little guys are the next best thing to cashews in the world of dairy-free delights. Because they're blanched, they are softer than a raw almond, and their skins are removed. This gives them the opportunity to transform into a creamy and luscious texture in milks, cheeses, and sauces.

Macadamia Nuts: This is a personal favorite of mine and probably the most indulgent choice on this entire list. Macadamia nuts grow in tropical climates and are incredibly fatty and flavorful. A little goes a long way, and although they are the pricier option, they are worth every penny.

Hazelnuts: Hazelnuts are more than just useful for your nutcracker. They can create the most delicious Vanilla Nut-Nog (page 58) and are the nuttiest flavor of all the nuts listed here. What I love most about hazelnuts is their nutrient profile, which is full of antioxidants and can dramatically decrease oxidative stress.

SEEDS

Hemp Seeds: Hemp seeds are the definition of a superfood. They have *so many* benefits nutritionally, and speaking from a chef's perspective, they are incredibly versatile. They're nutty and earthy, can be easily transformed, and can cling onto pretty much any flavor profile you give them. They are rich in plant protein and omega fatty acids.

Black Sesame Seeds: I like to have a bulk bag of black sesame seeds on hand at all times. They not only make for an epic crunchy addition to so many dishes but transform into an incredible milk (page 57). These are the key to watching you transform and glow from within, as they are so high in nutrients.

Sunflower Seeds: Another seed to help your skin glow from within! These seeds are packed with vitamin E. They can be transformed into a creamy cheese (see Pourable Mozzarella, page 88) and have the versatility power of cashews with a little added layer of nuttiness.

GRAINS AND BEANS

Oats: Oats are kind of like cauliflower in the vegan world; for so long, they were the boring, typical choice, but now they can transform into just about anything. They can be easily made into a very inexpensive milk, an allergy-friendly cheese, and the most epic GF flour substitute. It's almost as if they heard us call them boring and decided that this was the time they proved us wrong.

Firm and Silken Tofu: In the world of wellness culture, I'd say tofu gets a bad rap. I have a lot to say about soy and tofu, so buckle up because we are clearing this up once and for all.

First and foremost, I use tofu a lot in this book because it is such a perfect ingredient to create creamy textures. Tofu, itself, binds to literally any flavor you put on it or into it, so it's really such an easy ingredient to use even if you're new to the world of tofu! Second, tofu is one of the most cost-effective ingredients you'll find in this book, making it an obvious and accessible choice for anyone looking to give up dairy.

People will tell you that "tofu has estrogen" or that "tofu is causing deforestation" or that "tofu is highly processed and inflammatory." I'm here to tell you that all these things are incorrect and, in fact, couldn't be further from the truth. First, let's dive into tofu and estrogen. Tofu has a chemical called *phytoestrogen*, which isn't quite the same thing as the estrogen our body makes or the estrogen you would find in dairy. This phytoestrogen actually can be beneficial for reproductive health, as in regulating menstrual cycles; it also can help with blood sugar regulation and actually *reduce* your risk of breast cancer.

An incredibly common misconception is that the soy we eat is causing deforestation. Soy crops, themselves, are a huge cause for deforestation, but it's not what you think. Eighty percent of the soy grown in the world goes directly to feeding livestock. Four percent goes to biodiesel and lubricants. Fourteen percent is for oil and soy by-products for processed food. Only 7 percent of the total soy grown in the *entire world* goes to soybeans for eating, tofu, and tempeh. Tofu is not the problem here; animal agriculture is!

Finally, tofu is a *packaged* food, not a processed one. The caveat here is to make sure that you buy organic soy products whenever possible, as nonorganic soy products are some of the most heavily sprayed and genetically modified crops. The good news is that organic soy is still incredibly budget-friendly and available almost everywhere. Knowing all this info will help you fight misinformation and also help you feel better about what you're eating and making with the help of this book!

SEASONINGS

Miso Paste: Miso paste might seem like the ingredient you could live without, but in the vegan cheese world, let me just stop you right there and emphasize how crucial miso paste is for flavor. It is a fermented soybean paste that has a sweet, salty, and fermented flavor that can almost replicate the vibe of cheese when added. Don't skip this one!

Cacao: Mark my words, you will always see cacao instead of cocoa powder in this cookbook and every book I write from here on out. Cacao powder is made by fermenting the cacao plant, which yields an incredibly high amount of antioxidants and flavor. Cocoa is made by cooking the beans at a high temperature, which rids it of a lot of the nutrients and creates a duller flavor. Not to mention that the cacao brings the vibes and can actually make you feel like you're a little buzzed—it's *that* magical.

Lemon + White Wine Vinegar + Cider Vinegar: All three of these are a must-have in your home kitchen at all times. Whenever anything you make feels a little "flat" and it just isn't quite hitting right or isn't as bright as you wanted, my bet is it just needs a little zing to bring it back to life. That's where these three come into play. *Any* vinegar or citrus can do this, but for the sake of our breakup, these three are the ones you want.

Kelp Flakes: Kelp flakes are found near the spices and sometimes in the Asian section of the supermarket. Not only are these a great source of iodine, but kelp is the perfect addition to give anything the seafood vibe.

Probiotic Powder: Probiotic powder is most easily found inside probiotic capsules. It's a great little cheat way to add probiotics and good bacteria to recipes and to get the jump start on fermentation.

THE SPICE CABINET

This goes without saying, but a stocked spice cabinet will make your life so much easier when making delish recipes on the fly. The following are my must-haves for this book and, quite frankly, for life in general.

NUTRITIONAL YEAST	SMOKED PAPRIKA
TURMERIC	WHITE AND BLACK PEPPER
GARLIC POWDER	SALT
ONION POWDER	HERBS

GLUTEN-FREE FLOUR

We'll use a few gluten-free flours, such as cassava, oat, and 1-to-1 baking flour, throughout. When looking for a 1-to-1 baking flour, make sure the flour has a base of white or brown rice flour, some kind of starch, and xanthan gum. This trio will make for the perfect replacement to be sure that your recipe will work!

THICKENERS AND EMULSIFIERS

Potato Starch + Tapioca Starch: Starch is your BFF during this breakup. The ability it has to transform any sauce or cheese is nothing short of incredible and should not be taken lightly. Both of these should be in your pantry at all times because we use them a lot throughout this book. It's my favorite way to create the textures and consistencies we need. Starch plus plant fat equals the perfect substitute for the milk fat you find in cheeses and sauces. You might be thinking, *Bai, that sounds like magic*, but actually, it's just *science*.

Garbanzo Bean Flour: We use this one sparingly throughout the book, but it's worth mentioning because of how magical this ingredient is. Made from garbanzo beans (chickpeas), it has the ability to make the same magic as the starches while adding a really clean plant protein to the mix.

Agar-Agar: The world of plant cheese can be filled with some unconventional/unfamiliar thickening ingredients like rejuvelac and carrageenan. To make the cheese-making process a little more accessible, we opted for our favorite, which is agar-agar. Agar-agar is somewhat of the gelatin equivalent in the plant world. It is extracted from seaweed and turned into flakes and a powder. For this book, make sure to head online for this—buy powdered agar-agar, not flaked—and get a 4-ounce (115 g) bag to start!

Refined Coconut Oil: Refined coconut oil is such a game changer because, unlike pure coconut oil, it has absolutely no flavor. It's also less expensive, making it a win-win! I would definitely recommend buying this in bulk, as we use it for a few cheeses throughout the book.

Extra-Virgin Olive Oil: A little goes a long way with this ingredient. It's the easiest and most effective way to make any cheese or sauce silky smooth. Plus, it's such a vibe to cook onions in and transforms the entire dish from the first step. EVOO, you might just be the love of my life.

Plain Yogurt: Luckily, the store-bought plant yogurt world has come a long way in the last few years. I don't go into making our own in this book because I wanted to keep everything to a setting time of twelve hours or less; however, I do love the use of this ingredient to help bring a tang and thickness to cheeses and sauces.

Dates: Dates are actual gold mines in the world of plant milk. They're naturally sweet, so you don't have to add any extra sweetener, and they are the world's best thickening agent. These little nuggets are also rich in antioxidants.

SWEETENERS

Coconut Sugar: Coconut sugar is my preferred sweetener for so many reasons. The top two are that it's low on the glycemic index and it's one of the most eco-friendly options out there right now. It has a brown sugar–like taste and appearance, and can help you caramelize anything *seamlessly*.

Pure Maple Syrup + Date Syrup: These two can often be swapped for each other as they create a rich and velvety texture in anything you add them to. They are also not refined, making them an ideal choice for lowering inflammation in the body.

Agave Nectar: Agave nectar is the best unrefined neutral sweetener out there! Its pale color and neutral flavor make it an obvious choice for so many recipes. I love to buy agave in bulk at Costco to make sure my pantry is always stocked.

Organic Cane Sugar (Powdered): It wasn't until recently that I learned most conventional cane sugar is made by using bovine bone char (from cows) to "bleach" the sugar to make it snow-white. Unfortunately, dairy cows are often sent through the slaughterhouse after they are done being used for milk, and a common by-product is finding a way to use the bones. Buying certified organic is an easy way to make sure that no dairy cows—or any cows, for that matter—were harmed in the manufacturing of your sugar.

A New Wardrobe = a New You

The Beyoncé moment of this breakup is giving your kitchen supplies the revival they need, so you can coast effortlessly through the chapters of this book and into your new life without dairy.

I'm assuming you already have the basics like pots, pans, measuring spoons, and mixing bowls, so this list is everything you need that could be looked at as "extra" outside the basics. I ordered this list of supplies with the most important first, so you can budget and get what you need line by line without breaking the bank. It is safe to say you'll need all these things, but start from the top!

High-Powered Blender with Accelerator Stick: The nonnegotiable has entered the chat. A high-powered blender is a *must* for so many recipes in this book and you won't be able to make most of them without one! My go-to option that has the best warranty and the most bang for your buck is Vitamix. You can find refurbished ones for around $250, and they will last you for decades! If you're looking for something a little cheaper, it's important to make sure that the blades are on the bottom of the blender, and that there is an accelerator stick, which goes into the top of the blender while it's on, to keep things moving. Also, avoid the low- and wide-profile pitchers for the blender and opt for the classic, high-profile version. This will allow you to blend smaller-batch cheeses and sauces with ease! Cleanblend, Homgeek, Cosori, Brandless, and KitchenAid are all brands that have a similar style to Vitamix and are a bit more cost-effective.

Steamer Basket: Having a pot with a steamer basket attachment or a separate steamer basket will be crucial for many recipes in here. Steaming is one of my favorite methods for cheese making and softening ingredients while still keeping their integrity for flavor and texture.

Food Processor: As redundant as it sounds to have a high-powered blender and a food processor, they each serve their own purpose. Food processors have a wider bowl and can shred a drier product, making them a little bit more of a workhorse in the kitchen. If you were to choose one or the other, I would go with the blender first, as we have more blender-required recipes, and then have a food processor on your wish list after that!

Cheesecloth: Cheesecloth is a cotton fabric that we use consistently throughout the cheese chapter; it's one of the most effortless ways to get the perfect consistency from your cheese while it sets. The job of the cheesecloth is to absorb any extra moisture that the cheese gives off while it does its thing in the fridge. Not all the cheeses we make use a cheesecloth, but for the ones that do—it's a crucial step you can't skip! You can find cheesecloth very affordably at your grocery store or online.

Mason Jars with a Lid: Never underestimate the power of a mason jar. I have cabinets full of them because they are the easiest way to store so many things. I also love mason jars because they are super easy to sanitize and last so much longer than storing in plastic. Invest in some 16-ounce and 32-ounce jars. I would look at your local hardware store, as they always have the best prices on these, rather than shopping online.

Cheese Molds: Often in the cheese chapter, I'll ask you to pour or scoop the cheese you made into a mold. I personally love using 8-ounce square silicone molds, but Glasslock containers work well for this too! You can find both of these online.

Fine-Mesh Metal Strainer: This strainer will become your BFF during the milk chapter. I really wanted to avoid nut-milk straining bags as much as possible because I find it a little annoying and too messy. So my obvious answer and replacement is the fine-mesh metal strainer. You can find these anywhere and they'll help you get a supersmooth consistency for your milks without squeezing all you've got into a nut-milk straining bag.

Tofu Press: You can use a traditional tofu press, or you can wrap your drained tofu in a clean kitchen towel and put some books on top. I usually press for about 15 minutes. The goal here is to remove the water from the tofu, which will help make it denser and result in a better overall outcome for the recipe.

Nut-Milk Straining Bag: Okay, I know I just talked a little bit of smack about these, but you still will want to have one handy. Certain ingredients that are a little more fibrous will require this bag, but you won't use it much, promise.

Citrus Squeezer: This is one of those items that aren't fully necessary but will make your life so much easier. We squeeze a whole lot of lemons in this book and having a handheld citrus squeezer will become something you use every day, if you don't already have one. Again, you can usually find this at your local grocery for under $10, so pop this onto the list right next to that steamer basket.

There's Someone Out There for Everyone . . .

By now, you should be feeling so beyond ready to get started on your dairy-free journey and ready to jump in with both feet, without looking back. That said, I fully understand that there is an elephant in the room for some people, and that is wondering how this book will work with food allergies. It doesn't get past me how 68 percent of the global population is lactose intolerant (hence the inspo for this book), and also, there are millions of people with food allergies to nuts, grains, seeds, soy, and gluten.

I shifted my career from being a private chef who worked for high-end clients to being a chef for the average person because of food allergies and intolerances. There are so many boring and less-than-acceptable options for people with allergies, and I believe more than anything that they should have options for delicious food, no matter what allergy. I love the metaphor for dating for this because even though not every recipe in here will work for everyone, there is someone—and in this case a bomb recipe (or ten)—for everyone.

The following are some of the common allergen ingredients that are used throughout this book, and what you can use to replace them. I even listed the ingredients that can't be replaced, so you know that maybe a recipe just isn't for you. I've got you covered and I've thought about you and your kids too. Be sure to check each recipe for the allergens listed at the bottom of each page before you get started!

Cashews + Blanched Slivered Almonds + Sunflower Seeds: Throughout this book, you can replace cashews one-to-one with blanched slivered almonds and raw sunflower seeds. With blanched slivered almonds, the flavor will be really similar. With the sunflower seeds, the flavor will be a little earthier, but you'll still be able to achieve the textures and satisfy the cravings! The same goes, vice versa, for any of these three ingredients, so if you see blanched almonds listed, you can use cashews; or for sunflower seeds, you can use blanched almonds. I purposely determined the specific ingredients for each recipe to get the exact flavor I wanted, but that doesn't mean you can't play with it!

Tofu + Miso Paste: A one-to-one swap for tofu isn't quite as easy in our cheese and sauce recipes; however, you can now find garbanzo bean and fava bean tofu, and garbanzo bean miso paste, at stores like Whole Foods Market, and online. They will take a little extra digging to find, but I promise you, they're out there and a great replacement!

Nutritional Yeast: Nutritional yeast is a seasoning that helps give that cheesy flavor to so many dairy-free recipes. While using it really does help boost that flavor, if you have a yeast allergy or a reaction to nutritional yeast, you can just omit it!

Coconut Oil/Oil: As much as I wanted to make this entire book oil-free, it just wasn't hitting the mark from a flavor and texture perspective for a few of our cheeses and for the butter. If you are oil-free, just skip these recipes, as there are a lot of recipes that are oil-free!

Gluten: A vast majority of these recipes are GF or can be made GF. Look out for the suggested substitution, but if you don't see a "gluten-free" or "gluten-free optional" tag on the recipe, unfortunately, that recipe just isn't the same or worth your time and energy without the gluten.

PLANT-MILK HACK:
Because these recipes are oil-, gum-, filler-, and preservative-free, you'll need to shake each milk well to get everything nice and combined before enjoying out of the fridge. Shaking is also an easy way to foam up your coffee creamer to bring life back into it, even days after you make it! Also, don't forget the dates because they act as a natural thickener!

3. Don't CRY OVER SPILLED MILK

LUCKY FOR YOU, finding a plant-based milk that works for you (and your morning coffee) won't be a task that will end with tears. It seems that everyone has an opinion on which plant-based milk they like, or . . . don't like. This chapter is the be-all and end-all to every kind of dairy and not-so-dairy milk you can imagine. It has classics like almond and oat; personal favorites of mine, like raspberry horchata; and trends that are just getting started, like black sesame seed milk. This chapter doesn't skimp on milks you'll need for recipes, like sweetened condensed, and will even surprise you with an amaretto coffee creamer. All you need is some pantry ingredients, a blender, a strainer, and a mason jar to make this the lowest-maintenance search for love you'll ever have.

No-Strain ALMOND MILK

makes 36 ounces

Almond milk is such a staple in a dairy-free diet, but the whole process of straining through a nut-milk bag almost always has me preferring to skip it or just going with store-bought. So, in the name of simplicity, I've created a solution to make the creamiest almond milk with no straining bag required. The secret? Using blanched slivered almonds! These little guys are free of skins and softer than raw almonds, so they make an epic alternative to the original, all while creating a creamier end result with so much less baggage.

THE GOODS

4 large pitted Medjool dates
¾ cup (105 g) blanched slivered almonds
¼ teaspoon salt
4 cups (960 ml) water

THE METHOD

First, double-check your dates to make sure they're pitted. Pits have been known to sneak in, and they're no fun for the blender. Combine everything in a high-powered blender and blend on high speed for 1 to 3 minutes. Pour into a mason jar and refrigerate (I like this one nice and chilled). Enjoy within 5 to 7 days.

cashew-free

gluten-free

soy-free

grain-free

oil-free

Oat HEMP MILK

makes 34 ounces

Oat milk is the old reliable. The coffee shop GOAT. The mainstream dependable milk alternative. There is a caveat to creating the best oat milk at home because, although it seems so simple, it's pretty typical to get a slimy consistency, making most home cooks give up too easily. Hemp seeds help with the smooth consistency and are a no-brainer healthy protein and omega addition to this classic recipe. There's a trick to making the best oat milk, and that is the rule of "7 seconds." Usually it's considered a red flag if something takes only 7 seconds, but with this recipe you can get the *best* oat milk in exactly 7 seconds.

THE GOODS

4 cups (960 ml) water
⅓ cup (35 g) oats
2 tablespoons (20 g) hemp seeds
1 tablespoon (15 ml) date sugar or agave nectar
Pinch of salt

THE METHOD

Combine all the ingredients in a high-powered blender and blend on high speed for 7 seconds. Try not to blend for longer than 7 seconds, as it will make the milk slimy. Pour the milk mixture through a fine-mesh metal strainer into a bowl. Discard the leftover contents in the strainer, and then place the strainer over the blender. Pour and strain from the bowl back into the blender. For a super-creamy milk, repeat this straining process three times. Pour into a 32-ounce mason jar, store in your refrigerator, and enjoy within 4 to 6 days.

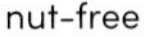
nut-free

gluten-free

soy-free

oil-free

makes 32 ounces

This is the *perfect* replacement for the traditional whole milk. The consistency, fat content, mouthfeel, and texture for recipes is literal perfection. The secret? Cashews, baby! And if you're worried about osteoporosis, cashews are an amazing source of copper, magnesium, and manganese, minerals that are responsible for building strong bones—which means they help prevent osteoporosis. The best part? They make the creamiest, smoothest, most delicious milk. It's a win-win.

***For more nutritional information on cashews, see page 31.**

THE GOODS

1 cup (140 g) cashews, soaked in hot water for 15 minutes, then drained
2 pitted Medjool dates
Pinch of pink salt
3 cups (720 ml) filtered water

THE METHOD

Simply combine everything in a high-powered blender and blend on high speed for 60 seconds. Pour into a 32-ounce jar and store in the fridge for 5 to 7 days. Use it as a heavy cream or whole milk replacement in your favorite recipes. Or dunk a cookie into it.

gluten-free

soy-free

grain-free

oil-free

NO
GUMS
NO
BINDERS
NO
PRESERVATIVES

Coconut MILK

makes 28 ounces

I'm well aware that it is *so* easy to buy a can of coconut milk, but making your own will help you avoid the added gums and fillers that can be a nightmare for digestion, and honestly, it tastes so much better freshly made. You can find coconut meat in the freezer section or packaged in the refrigerator produce section, or you can use unsweetened shredded dried coconut meat from the baking section of the grocery store. Either way, you'll get the silkiest, creamiest, and most delicious coconut milk made from scratch. No climbing a palm tree required.

THE GOODS

1 cup (120 g) coconut meat, or 1 cup (65 g) unsweetened shredded coconut
3 cups (720 ml) water
3 pitted Medjool dates
Pinch of salt

THE METHOD

Combine everything in a high-powered blender and blend on high speed for a minute. Pour the contents through a fine-mesh metal strainer and use a wooden spoon to help the liquid through. Repeat this straining process two more times. (If you want, you can also strain it once through a nut-milk straining bag.) Store in an airtight container, in the fridge, for 5 to 7 days. This milk works best with curries, lattes, and any recipe you want a thick and fatty milk for! It's also an incredible replacement for my Whole Milk (page 46).

cashew-free

gluten-free

soy-free

grain-free

oil-free

Blood Orange ICE CREAM MILK

makes 48 ounces

Your inner child is about to be jumping for joy with this recipe. It has all the elements of a Creamsicle . . . tangy, sweet, and oh-so-creamy. Turn this into ice cubes and blend for an epic milkshake, or pour over vegan vanilla ice cream, or better yet, pour into ice pop molds to freeze for the perfect late-night snack.

THE GOODS

3 cups (720 ml) water
1 cup (240 ml) blood orange juice
1 cup (140 g) cashews, soaked in hot water for 15 minutes, then drained
¼ cup (60 ml) pure maple syrup
3 tablespoons (45 ml) Coconut Milk (page 49), or canned
2 pitted Medjool dates
2 teaspoons pure vanilla extract
Pinch of salt

THE METHOD

Combine everything in a high-powered blender and blend on high speed for 60 seconds. Strain the liquid through a fine-mesh metal strainer into a large bowl. Pour into and store in an airtight container (I like to use two 32-ounce mason jars) in the fridge. Best enjoyed within 6 days. Shake before serving.

gluten-free soy-free grain-free oil-free

Granola MILK

makes 36 ounces

If the munchies had a love affair with a type of milk, it would 100 percent be this one. Imagine you are eating a huge bowl of your favorite cereal, and when you finish the cereal, all that's left is the delicious milk at the bottom that's slightly sweet and toasted . . . that's the entire vibe of this recipe in a jar! This granola milk is the perfect treat or coffee creamer. It's also incredible in a milkshake (see tip) and will easily become the new family favorite milk to keep on hand.

THE GOODS

¼ cup (35 g) cashews
2 tablespoons (20 g) hulled sunflower seeds
2 tablespoons (10 g) shredded coconut
2 tablespoons (12 g) coconut sugar (sub cane sugar for coconut allergy)
2 tablespoons (30 g) unsalted almond butter
3 pitted Medjool dates
4 cups (960 ml) filtered water

THE METHOD

① Preheat the oven to 350°F (177°C). Line a small baking dish with parchment paper and set aside.

② Combine the cashews, sunflower seeds, shredded coconut, coconut sugar, and almond butter in a small bowl. Use a rubber spatula to press all the nuts, seeds, and coconut sugar into the almond butter, making sure everything is well incorporated.

③ Transfer your granola to the prepared lined baking dish and bake for 10 minutes. After 10 minutes, remove from the oven and stir, then bake again for 4 to 5 minutes.

④ Transfer the granola to a high-powered blender, add the dates and filtered water, and blend on high speed for 45 to 60 seconds. Use a fine-mesh metal strainer to strain the milk into a bowl, then transfer the milk to a clean 32-ounce mason jar and store in the fridge for 5 to 7 days.

tip * **Freeze half a batch into ice cubes to make the Granola Cookie Dough Milkshake (page 267).**

gluten-free

soy-free

grain-free

oil-free

Pistachio MILK

makes 32 ounces

The passenger princess within us all is in desperate need of this perfectly creamy and decadent milk. Pistachios are the perfect base for the best latte milk you'll ever have in your life. Picture this: sitting in the passenger seat, with a frothy pistachio latte in one hand, the window's down, and the sight of your nasty breakup is in the rearview mirror. All that's left is to put on your favorite song, sit back, and enjoy what lies ahead.

THE GOODS

½ cup (65 g) shelled pistachios, soaked in hot water for 15 minutes, then drained
4 cups (960 ml) water
2 pitted Medjool dates
2 teaspoons coconut sugar (sub cane sugar for coconut allergy)
¼ teaspoon ground cinnamon
Pinch of salt

THE METHOD

Combine all the ingredients in a high-powered blender and blend on high speed for 45 to 60 seconds. Pour through a fine-mesh metal strainer into a bowl and then transfer to a mason jar or container with a tight seal. Store in the fridge and serve chilled. Best enjoyed before 7 days. ***Did I mention this is perfect for lattes?!***

cashew-free

gluten-free

soy-free

grain-free

oil-free

Black Sesame SEED MILK

makes 32 ounces

We love a milk that can cross cultures and create a beautiful umami flavor. Black sesame seed milk is the perfect example of how creating "milk" from plants can provide limitless possibilities and make life so much more interesting than it was before. It can make a silky-smooth ramen broth (page 191), and is the perfect addition to the creamy flan (page 272). Want to make this without breaking the bank? Buy black sesame seeds online in bulk, and you can get a 2-pound bag for the same price you would get 2 to 4 ounces at your local grocery store.

THE GOODS

- ½ cup (60 g) black sesame seeds
- 4 cups (960 ml) filtered water
- 1 teaspoon pure vanilla extract
- 4 pitted Medjool dates
- ¼ teaspoon salt

THE METHOD

Combine all the ingredients in a high-powered blender and blend on high speed for about 60 seconds, or until well mixed. Pour through a fine-mesh metal strainer into a bowl. You might need to work a rubber spatula on the strainer to help the liquid go through. Repeat this one more time to get a really smooth consistency. This milk pairs amazingly for a matcha latte.

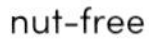
nut-free

gluten-free

soy-free

grain-free

oil-free

Vanilla NUT-NOG

makes 32 ounces

'Tis the season to be naughty, or nice, or whatever you want. Either way, it's the season to officially start making your own Nut-Nog. Make it boozy and class it up with some coffee and Licor 43, or add it to the Vanilla Nut-Nog Tres Leches Cake (page 299). This baddie is thick enough to be a coffee creamer and will knock the socks off any eggnog-loving friend you want to share this with. Move over, eggnog; there's a new hottie in town.

THE GOODS

1 cup (120 g) hazelnuts
3 cups (720 ml) water
6 pitted Medjool dates
1 tablespoon (15 ml) pure maple syrup
½ teaspoon pure vanilla extract
1 teaspoon ground cinnamon
½ teaspoon ground ginger
¼ teaspoon ground cloves
¼ teaspoon ground cardamom
Pinch of nutmeg

THE METHOD

① Preheat the oven to 300°F (150°C). Spread the hazelnuts on a baking sheet and bake for 10 minutes. Remove from the oven and let cool for 5 minutes.

② Combine the hazelnuts and water in a high-powered blender. Blend on high speed for 2 minutes. Pour the mixture through a nut-milk straining bag over a large bowl, squeezing the pulp to extract as much liquid as you can. Alternatively, you can use a fine-mesh metal strainer—but if you do, you will have to strain it quite a few times with this method.

③ Transfer the liquid back to your blender and add the rest of the ingredients. Blend on high speed for 2 minutes. Transfer to a 32-ounce mason jar. The nut-nog will stay delicious in your fridge for 5 to 7 days. Shake before serving. I prefer it chilled, but it's also delicious served over ice or as a coffee creamer, fresh out of the blender.

cashew-free

gluten-free

soy-free

grain-free

oil-free

Lazy Girl's BARISTA SOY MILK

makes 40 ounces

There's nothing quite like the love affair I have with sleeping in, drinking coffee, and staying in my bathrobe all morning long. Nothing can compare to the satisfaction of having absolutely nothing on the schedule until after noon. With the spirit of the lazy gal within, this high-protein creamy milk is as easy as throwing everything into a blender and turning it on. It froths perfectly in a milk frother and never did I ever think a homemade cappuccino would be so easy and so dang good.

THE GOODS

12 ounces (340 g) silken tofu
3 cups (720 ml) water
3 pitted Medjool dates
1 tablespoon (15 ml) pure maple syrup
½ teaspoon ground cinnamon
Pinch of salt

THE METHOD

Combine all the ingredients in a high-powered blender and blend on medium-high speed for 45 seconds. When you turn off the blender, the mixture will be a bit foamy, so you can skim away the top foam layer. Store in an airtight container in the fridge and consume within 2 to 3 days. Shake well before using.

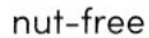
nut-free

gluten-free

grain-free

oil-free

All Things HORCHATA

makes 36 ounces creamer; 48 ounces straight up

Horchata is one of my all-time favorite beverages to drink over ice or as a perfect pairing for an iced coffee. But kind of like dating, ordering horchata out in the world is always a gamble; it's hard to *really know* if it's deliciously dairy-free or packed with heavy cream. This horchata recipe is not only a perfect match, but it has a flavor to go with every mood, season, and phase. If you're looking to elevate things, the Espresso Horchata is the move on a Sunday morning, paired with the Raspberry Horchata Fluffy Pancakes (page 148). There just isn't a better hangover cure or a better way to start off the best day of the week. The ultimate hack to get the *creamiest* horchata is to make sure you soak your rice in very hot water for an hour rather than letting it soak overnight or cooking it on the stove. *Salud!*

THE GOODS

Coffee Creamer:

½ cup (100 g) uncooked white rice, soaked in hot water for 1 hour
4 pitted Medjool dates
¼ cup (60 ml) agave nectar
½ teaspoon ground cinnamon
3 cups (720 ml) water
½ cup (120 ml) coconut cream or full-fat coconut milk

Pour Over Ice:

Coffee Creamer ingredients + 1 more cup (240 ml) water

Chocolate Horchata:

All the Pour Over Ice ingredients + ¼ cup (15 g) unsweetened cacao powder and 2 tablespoons (30 ml) more agave nectar

Raspberry Horchata:

All the Pour Over Ice ingredients + ¾ cup (80 g) fresh raspberries

Espresso Horchata:

All the Pour Over Ice ingredients + 4 teaspoons espresso powder

recipe continues →

nut-free

gluten-free

soy-free

oil-free

THE METHOD

For Coffee Creamer or Pour Over Ice:
Place the soaked rice in a strainer and give it a good rinse. Combine all the ingredients for either version in a high-powered blender and blend on medium-high speed for 60 to 90 seconds, or until everything is well mixed, smooth, and creamy. Strain three times through a fine-mesh metal strainer or pour through a nut-milk straining bag once. Pour into an airtight container and store in the refrigerator for 4 to 6 days . . . if it lasts that long.

For Chocolate, Raspberry, or Espresso Horchata:
Place the soaked rice in a strainer and give it a good rinse. Combine all the ingredients, except the cacao, raspberry, or espresso powder, in a high-powered blender and blend on medium-high speed for 60 to 90 seconds, or until everything is well mixed, smooth, and creamy. Strain three times through a fine-mesh metal strainer or pour once through a nut-milk straining bag. Pour back into the blender and add your flavor! Blend for 30 seconds, pour into your mason jars, and then store in the refrigerator for 4 to 6 days. You will need to shake well before enjoying.

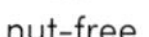
nut-free

gluten-free

soy-free

oil-free

Amaretto COFFEE CREAMER

makes 36 ounces

This is giving bougie coffee-date-off-the-Santorini-coastline. It's giving a mental Italian vacation brought to your taste buds on a coffee vessel. Store-bought coffee creamers *wish* they could be this incredibly perfect. You actually don't need amaretto for this one. Who knew that almond butter + cherries + dates + vanilla = foamy, luscious, and perfectly sweet creamer? I guess it's real when they say that true love is often right in front of you the whole time and you didn't even realize it.

THE GOODS

½ cup (120 g) almond butter
2 pitted Medjool dates
3 tablespoons (35 g) coconut sugar (sub organic cane sugar for coconut allergy)
4 or 5 (20 g) frozen pitted cherries
1 teaspoon pure vanilla extract
4 cups (960 ml) water

THE METHOD

Combine all the ingredients in a high-powered blender and blend on high speed for a minute. The creamer should be foamy and perfectly blended. I personally love to immediately pour this blend into my coffee to capitalize on all that luscious foam. Store the rest in a mason jar in the fridge. Be sure to thoroughly enjoy it within 7 days and to shake well before serving.

Instant Single-Serving CHOCOLATE MILK + HOT CHOCOLATE

makes one 18-ounce serving

Nothing says a perfect solo treat like 10 teaspoons of refined sugar, corn syrup, highly processed milk fat, preservatives, and artificial flavoring . . . just kidding! However, those are the most common ingredients of the most popular single-serving chocolate milks and hot chocolate milks on the shelves. This single-serving cold or hot chocolate milk is made up of whole ingredients that you can find in your pantry, which will not only satisfy your craving but give your body plant protein, antioxidants, and magnesium. Heal through hot chocolate? Oh yeah.

THE GOODS

4 pitted Medjool dates
2 tablespoons (10 g) unsweetened cacao powder
2 cups (480 ml) water
¼ cup (65 g) almond butter
Pinch of salt

THE METHOD

Combine all the ingredients in a high-powered blender and blend on high speed for 60 seconds, or until everything is fully smooth. Pour over ice into a large glass and serve immediately. If you wish to enjoy hot, pour the blend into a saucepan and heat for about 2 minutes over medium heat. Store in the fridge for 3 to 4 days. Shake well before using.

cashew-free

gluten-free

soy-free

grain-free

oil-free

Sweetened Condensed OAT MILK

makes 10 ounces

The perfect match if you have a food allergy or are looking for a low-fat, heart-healthy alternative to sweetened condensed cow's or coconut milk. This is a year-round must-have on your meal prep roster, from the Orange Cold-Brew Rumtini (page 254) to holiday cookie bars to Brazilian lemonade (*limonada suíça*). Oat milk is the perfect base for this sweetened condensed milk because the oats act as a binder, which creates a glossy and smooth texture. Say bye to the canned store-bought and hello to a budget-friendly, delicious alternative that everyone can enjoy.

THE GOODS

- 2 cups (480 ml) Oat Hemp Milk (page 45)
- ½ cup (120 ml) pure maple syrup

THE METHOD

Combine the oat hemp milk and maple syrup in a small saucepan and whisk until fully mixed. Place the saucepan over medium heat. Cook for 20 to 25 minutes, stirring occasionally. Do not walk away from this as it can and will bubble over the sides if you are not careful. Just stir and lower the heat if it gets too hot or bubbly—it will depend on the size of your burner and pan. The liquid should reduce by half, and you'll be left with a glossy, smooth, and thick finish. Remove from the heat, let cool completely, then store in an airtight container in the refrigerator. It will thicken a bit more as it cools down. If you decide to double the recipe, you will need to increase the cooking time to 35 to 40 minutes. Best enjoyed within 5 to 6 days.

nut-free

gluten-free

soy-free

oil-free

No Whey! Chocolate PROTEIN POWDER

makes twelve ¼-cup (25 g) servings

Nothing says *revenge body* like effortlessly meeting your protein and chocolate needs every day. This No-Whey! protein powder is such an epic way to get your protein (11 g per serving!), omegas, antioxidants, and healthy fats without any of the BS that is in most protein powders. You get everything your body needs while saying goodbye to the bloat, acne, fatigue, and headaches that can pair with traditional powdered and processed whey. You can find most of these ingredients in bulk online, and although it's a bit of an investment to get stocked up, you'll be able to make many, *many* batches of this with just one online order and save a whole lot of money over time. You can also adjust the recipe to meet your protein needs or to sweeten it so it's perfect for you, and your revenge bod too.

THE GOODS

- 1 cup (125 g) pea protein powder
- ½ cup (90 g) coconut milk powder
- ½ cup (35 g) unsweetened cacao powder
- ½ cup (80 g) coconut sugar (for a sweeter powder, add an extra ¼ cup of coconut sugar)
- 2 tablespoons (15 g) flaxseed meal
- 2 tablespoons (10 g) ground chia seeds

THE METHOD

Using a sifter, sift all the ingredients, except the flaxseed meal and ground chia seeds, into a large bowl, then add the flaxseed meal and ground chia seeds and stir with a dry fork or whisk until everything is fully mixed. Store in a large, dry, airtight container in a dark area of the kitchen away from sunlight. To serve, blend ¼ cup (25 g) of No Whey! powder with 1½ cups (355 ml) of plant-based milk or water, and enjoy immediately. This is a great addition to smoothies or a base for chia pudding.

cashew-free

gluten-free

soy-free

grain-free

oil-free

Hibiscus REFRESHER

makes two 16-ounce refreshers

Nothing says bouncing back from a breakup like taking yourself on a much-needed vacay. Although this recipe won't quite get you all the way to the Maldives, it's pretty damn close. Whether you're in a NYC apartment, a cottage in the country, or on the beach in San Diego, this mocktail, with hints of mango, coconut, and lime, will transport you to a vacation state of mind. Hibiscus tea is the perfect addition, as it can lower your blood pressure (say goodbye to stress), can help reduce inflammation in the body, and is packed with antioxidants. It's a reminder that vacations (and, quite frankly, life) are best spent with those who make you feel nothing short of amazing.

THE GOODS

- 9 ounces (265 ml) brewed hibiscus tea
- 1.5 ounces (45 ml) agave nectar
- 3 ounces (85 ml) freshly squeezed lime juice
- ¼ cup (40 g) chopped mango
- 1½ cups (180 g) ice + more for the glasses
- 6 ounces Coconut Milk (page 49)

THE METHOD

Prep two 16-ounce glasses by filling with ice and set aside. In a cocktail shaker, combine the tea, agave nectar, lime juice, mango, and ice. Pop the lid on and shake well for about a minute. Really shake hard to get all the juice out of the mango. Using the strainer lid on the cocktail shaker (or a fine-mesh metal strainer), strain the liquid into both glasses, leaving some room at the top. Garnish each glass with 3 ounces of coconut milk. Enjoy immediately while the ice is fresh.

cashew-free

gluten-free

soy-free

grain-free

oil-free

4. The One You CAN'T LIVE WITHOUT

I'VE SAID IT, YOU'VE SAID IT, and at some point, we've all meant it. "I could never give up cheese." I get it, entire civilizations and cultures were built on the stuff. I spent my entire chef career thinking about it. Before I broke up with dairy, I was thinking about cheese all the time—ordering cheese boards, spending all my money on the good stuff, and spending way too many nights bingeing on quesadillas, pizzas, and grilled cheeses. I went to Le Cordon Bleu and lived right next door to wine country. Cheese was everywhere, and I couldn't get enough of it. Ever since I broke up with dairy, I find myself, even still, constantly thinking about cheese. But in a new, and I like to think in a more evolved, save-the-planet kind of way.

This chapter is an ode to cheese. It's a reminder that we can have our cheese and eat it too. It's proof that plants can work miracles, and with the help of a blender and some TLC, you're just a few hours away from a cheese board that doesn't make you bloat and a mozzarella that is what dreams are made of. We're making stinky cheese like Gorgonzola, game-time cheese like spicy nacho, refined cheese like Brie, and a personal fave that's one of the GOATs . . . well, it's my own version of goat cheese . . . See what I did there?

Herbed FARMER CHEESE

makes 20 ounces (2½ cups)

The concept of the farmer cheese hits different when the farmer is speaking my love language by growing almonds instead of raising cattle. This is the cheese that checks all the boxes, without the baggage. It's quick to make, incredibly flavorful (it's not called "herbed" for nothing), perfect for beginners, and completely oil-free. This is perfect for sandwiches, cheese boards, wraps, and on a baguette with an heirloom tomato for happy hour.

THE GOODS

- 1 garlic bulb, or 1½ teaspoons (5 g) granulated garlic
- 1 teaspoon olive oil, if roasting garlic
- ½ to 1 teaspoon salt
- 2 cups (240 g) blanched slivered almonds
- 1 tablespoon (2 g) fresh or dried rosemary, minced
- 1 tablespoon (2 g) fresh or dried oregano, minced
- 1½ teaspoons (1 g) dried thyme
- 1½ teaspoons (1 g) dried dill
- 1 cup (240 ml) No-Strain Almond Milk (page 42) or store-bought unsweetened almond milk
- 1 tablespoon (20 g) mellow white miso paste
- ¼ teaspoon freshly ground black pepper

THE METHOD

① If using a garlic bulb, preheat the oven to 350°F (177°C). Slice off and discard the top of the garlic bulb. Place the garlic bulb, cut side up, in an oven-safe dish. Drizzle with the olive oil and sprinkle with ½ teaspoon of the salt. Bake for 20 minutes. Once the garlic is soft and golden brown on the top, remove from the oven and let cool before using.

② If you roasted the garlic, squeeze the garlic from the bulb into a high-powered blender. Add the rest of ingredients, including the remaining ½ teaspoon of salt. If using granulated garlic instead, combine it with the remaining ingredients, including 1 teaspoon of salt, in a high-powered blender and blend on high speed, using an accelerator stick, for 45 to 60 seconds, or until you have a smooth consistency. Remove the lid and scrape down the excess cheese from the sides of the blender, then blend again for 45 to 60 seconds. Taste to make sure all the almonds have blended; there should be no large pieces. Serve immediately in a serving dish as a spread or, for a firmer cheese, let sit, in a Glasslock container, in the fridge for 2 to 6 hours. Store in an airtight container in the fridge and within before 7 days.

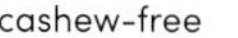
cashew-free

gluten-free

grain-free

oil-free

High-Protein COTTAGE CHEESE

makes 5 servings

The cottage cheese craze is back and, frankly, I'm hyped about it! When you think about it, it's somewhat a bizarre way to serve milk + milk fat together, but I absolutely love this plant-based version and I find it to be a little less bizarre. This version is packed with probiotics and plant protein, making it the perfect addition to any breakfast or pasta dish. The '90s are back, baby, and so is cottage cheese.

THE GOODS

1 (14-ounce [400 g]) block firm tofu, drained
1 teaspoon salt
½ cup (130 g) unsweetened, unflavored coconut yogurt
¾ cup (180 ml) Coconut Milk (page 49), No-Strain Almond Milk (page 42), or store-bought unsweetened plant-based milk of choice
1 teaspoon nutritional yeast
1 tablespoon (15 ml) freshly squeezed lemon juice

THE METHOD

① Slice off one-quarter of the block of tofu. Place that quarter-block in a high-powered blender along with the salt, coconut yogurt, coconut milk, nutritional yeast, and lemon juice. Blend on high speed until smooth, about 30 seconds. Transfer the mixture to a medium-size bowl. Crumble the remaining three-quarter block of tofu into little pieces and add to the bowl. These are going to be the "cheese curds," so crumble them to your preferred size. I enjoy large curds, so I crumble the tofu into larger pieces. Mix until well combined and boom—super-easy and yummy cottage cheese!

② Best enjoyed really cold, so be sure to refrigerate for at least an hour before eating. Enjoy within 6 days.

cashew-free

gluten-free

grain-free

oil-free

CREAM CHEESE

Makes one 16-ounce container

My dad always taught me to settle for nothing less than what I deserve, and he also taught me that any decent bagel deserves a ridiculous amount of cream cheese. There is no such thing as too much, especially in the eyes of a New Yorker. This cream cheese is lusciously smooth, high in plant protein, so versatile, and I even added a few flavors to try on, so you can find the flavor that vibes the best with you. Remember, it's not just cream cheese; it's the magic that makes a bagel worth eating.

THE GOODS

Plain:
- 1½ cups (210 g) cashews, soaked in hot water for 10 minutes, then drained
- ¼ cup (40 g) cooked or canned great northern beans
- ¼ cup (60 ml) melted refined coconut oil
- ¼ teaspoon salt
- 3 tablespoons (45 ml) freshly squeezed lemon juice
- 1 tablespoon (20 g) miso paste
- 1 tablespoon (15 ml) water

Strawberry Cheesecake:
- 5 strawberries, hulled
- 1 teaspoon pure vanilla extract
- 2 tablespoons (30 ml) pure maple syrup

Roasted Garlic + Scallion:
- 1 garlic bulb
- 1 teaspoon olive oil
- ¾ teaspoon salt
- 3 tablespoons (45 ml) freshly squeezed lemon juice
- 3 scallions, thinly sliced

THE METHOD

Plain or Strawberry Cheesecake: Combine all the ingredients for the plain cream cheese version, or the plain + strawberry cheesecake ingredients for the sweet version, in a high-powered blender and blend on medium speed for 1 to 2 minutes, or until fully smooth. You may need to use the accelerator stick to get things moving. Store in an airtight container for 5 to 7 days. Use on your favorite toast, in your favorite Danish (the one on page 150), or as dessert.

Roasted Garlic + Scallion: Preheat the oven to 350°F (177°C). Slice off and discard the top of the garlic bulb. Place the garlic bulb, cut side up, in an oven-safe dish. Drizzle with the olive oil and ½ teaspoon of the salt and bake for 20 minutes. Once the garlic is soft and golden brown on the top, remove from the oven and let cool. Squeeze the garlic from the bulb into a high-powered blender and add the plain cream cheese ingredients, lemon juice, and the remaining ¼ teaspoon of salt, and blend for 1 to 2 minutes, or until fully smooth. You may need to use the accelerator stick to get things moving. Remove the lid and add the sliced scallions, then pulse four to six times, or just until pieces of scallion are distributed throughout. (If you blend it too much, it will turn into a green mixture, which you don't want . . . unless that's want you do want. You do you.) Let it set for at least 4 hours before enjoying. Store in an airtight container for 5 to 7 days.

gluten-free

soy-free optional

grain-free

The Family-Size CHEDDAR BLOCK

makes one 16-ounce block

It's no secret that American culture has an extremely codependent relationship with Cheddar cheese. Even my parents hide a huge block of Cheddar in the back of the fridge and give me a blank stare when I find it on my visits. Because of this cultural obsession with this cheese, I made it my personal mission to create an incredible replacement. This recipe shreds, slices, melts, and does everything you want a Cheddar block to do. And because we are *so* obsessed as a culture with Cheddar, I made sure to supersize this one, so you never run out.

THE GOODS

- 2 small (180 g total) yellow potatoes, chopped
- 4 garlic cloves, peeled
- ⅔ cup (100 g) cashews
- 2 tablespoons (40 g) miso paste
- 2 tablespoons (10 g) nutritional yeast
- 1 teaspoon onion powder
- ½ teaspoon ground white pepper
- 2 teaspoons salt
- ¼ cup (60 ml) carrot juice
- ½ cup (80 g) potato starch
- ⅔ cup (160 ml) refined coconut oil

THE METHOD

① Set a steamer basket above a few inches of water in a large, lidded pot. Bring to a boil over medium heat. Place the potatoes, garlic, and cashews in the steamer basket, cover, and steam until fork-tender, for 10 to 15 minutes. Once tender, remove from the heat, transfer the veggies to a plate, and set aside to cool completely. You can place them in the fridge to speed up this process. Once cooled, combine the cooled veggies, cashews, and the rest of the ingredients in a high-powered blender and blend on medium speed until nice and smooth, for 1 to 2 minutes.

② Leaving the steamer basket and water in the pot, transfer the mixture from the blender to a silicone mold or heat-resistant Glasslock container without the lid; be sure to use a skinny blender spatula to help remove all the cheese from the blender; every drop counts. Place the mold or container in the steamer, cover the pot, and steam the cheese for 20 minutes over medium heat, then remove from the steamer and let cool for 30 minutes. Cover and refrigerate for at least 4 hours. Enjoy cold right out of the fridge. Melt it on everything!

gluten-free

soy-free optional

oil-free

Pourable MOZZARELLA

makes 18 ounces

Like most things related to matters of the heart, if it seems to be too good to be true, it usually is, but not in this case. You get everything you need from this pourable mozzarella, without any hard work and just a quick trip to your pantry. This mozz is as easy as adding everything to a blender and pouring it over your favorite dish or on top of a dish where you want a golden-brown layer of melted cheese. See it in action for the One-Pot Meyer Lemon Cacio e Pepe (page 184) and browned to perfection on the French Onion Fungi Soup (page 163).

THE GOODS

1 cup (140 g) cashews or hulled sunflower seeds, soaked in water for 15 minutes, then drained
1¼ cups (300 ml) water
½ teaspoon garlic powder
½ teaspoon salt
1 teaspoon nutritional yeast
1 teaspoon miso paste
3 tablespoons (20 g) tapioca starch

THE METHOD

Combine all the ingredients in a high-powered blender, and blend on high speed for 1 to 2 minutes, or until fully smooth. This is ready to go on your favorite pizza, pasta bake, grilled cheese, or to be part of a filling, such as in enchiladas or lasagna. Please note: This cheese does need to be cooked into something for at least 5 minutes or under the broiler; avoid consuming uncooked as a topping. Store in an airtight container in the fridge for 5 to 7 days.

nut-free optional

gluten-free

soy-free optional

grain-free

oil-free

ml 500
400
300
200

1/2 Tsp/2.5ml

PEPPER JACK

makes one 10-ounce block

When looking for the perfect match, there's a list of requirements that must be met. In the world of cheese, it must shred, slice, and melt. This pepper jack hits all of them while also being free of the top allergens. We've entered the world where you *can* have it all without sacrificing what you need and want out of a cheese. This is perfect for quesadillas, enchiladas, sandwiches, or just eating by the slice! For the perfect shred, freeze for fifteen minutes before taking to a cheese grater.

THE GOODS

- 2 tablespoons (15 g) tapioca starch
- 3 tablespoons (45 ml) water
- 1 cup (240 ml) Oat Hemp Milk (page 45) or store-bought unsweetened plant-based milk of choice
- 1 tablespoon (15 ml) olive oil
- 1 tablespoon (15 ml) white wine vinegar
- 1 tablespoon (10 g) agar-agar
- 1 teaspoon garlic powder
- 1 teaspoon onion powder
- ¾ teaspoon salt
- 2 tablespoons (10 g) nutritional yeast
- ¼ cup (40 g) garbanzo bean (chickpea) flour
- ¼ cup (40 g) seeded and minced red bell pepper
- 1 tablespoon (10 g) seeded and minced jalapeño

THE METHOD

① Line a 5 x 5-inch Glasslock container with enough cheesecloth, draped over the outer sides, to later cover the top, and set aside. Combine the tapioca starch and water in a small bowl. Mix until you get a paste, then set aside.

② Combine the oat milk, olive oil, and white wine vinegar in a medium-size saucepan. Whisk together over medium-low heat until well mixed and starting to get hot, but not boiling. Whisk in the agar-agar, garlic powder, onion powder, salt, nutritional yeast, garbanzo bean flour, bell pepper, and jalapeño. Keep whisking constantly for 2 to 4 minutes, or until the mixture starts to bubble and thicken. Quickly whisk in the tapioca paste until the mixture becomes superthick, for 1 to 2 minutes. Remove from the heat, and use a rubber spatula to scoop the mixture into your prepared container. Fold the extra cheesecloth over the top. Let chill for 6 hours or overnight before enjoying. Will keep for a week in the fridge in an airtight container.

nut-free

gluten-free

soy-free

grain-free optional

Young GRUYÈRE

makes one 5-inch wheel

The days I was in culinary school at Le Cordon Bleu were my most obsessive cheese days. At the very least, I would call it a codependent relationship. I even snagged a few very large blocks of Gruyère into my bag to eat when no one else was looking. These were the peak moments of my "I could never give up cheese" mindset. I created this recipe with my younger self in mind and for anyone else who is there too. This cheese hits so many similar flavor markers of Gruyère while having its own vibe by being soft and approachable to make. It proves once and for all that you *can* live a delicious and fulfilled life without an entire block of dairy Gruyère in your bag.

THE GOODS

½ batch Indulgent Queen Crema (page 129)
1 tablespoon (20 g) miso paste
1½ teaspoons (7.5 ml) sauerkraut juice
¼ cup (40 g) potato starch
2 tablespoons (10 g) nutritional yeast
¼ teaspoon salt

THE METHOD

Combine all the ingredients in a high-powered blender and blend on high speed for a minute. Pour the mixture into a Glasslock container, without the lid, or cheese mold. Set a large steamer basket above a few inches of water in a large, lidded pot, and place the container or mold, uncovered, in the steamer basket. Cover the pot and steam the cheese over medium heat for 30 minutes. Remove from the steamer and let cool completely, cover, then store in the fridge overnight or for at least 6 hours, or until set. Will keep in the fridge for 7 to 8 days.

gluten-free

soy-free optional

oil-free

Potato PARMESAN

makes one 14-ounce block

When I pulled the first block of this Parmesan out of the fridge, I knew I had found the Prince Charming of the dairy-free cheese world. This cheese tastes, shreds, and melts like an aged Parmesan, but it's made from potatoes and set in just 6 hours. Maybe it's a little bit of magic, or just maybe I've turned into a fairy godmother. Either way, look no further because we've found the one we've been looking for all along.

THE GOODS

- 1 cup (150 g) peeled, chopped potatoes
- ⅓ cup (80 ml) refined coconut oil, melted
- ¼ cup (40 g) potato starch
- 1½ teaspoons salt
- 1 tablespoon (15 ml) sauerkraut juice

THE METHOD

① Set a large steamer basket above a few inches of water in a large, lidded pot. Bring to a boil over medium heat. Add your potatoes to the steamer basket and steam until fork-tender, for about 15 minutes. Remove the potatoes (leaving the steamer basket and water in the pot, as you will be using them later) and let cool completely. **Do not skip this step, as it's essential.** If you're in a rush, you can pop them into the freezer for a few minutes to cool them quickly. They should be at room temperature and a little dry to the touch. Cooling them off allows the water content to reduce from the steam that is releasing from the potatoes.

② Once the potatoes are cool, combine them with the remaining ingredients in a high-powered blender and blend on high speed for 1 to 2 minutes. You might need to use the accelerator stick to get it moving. Set aside.

③ Reheat the water in the pot that contains the steamer basket. Meanwhile, pour the potato mixture into a silicone cheese mold or a heat-resistant glass container. Carefully place the mold into the steamer basket and cover the pot. Steam over medium-low heat for 13 to 14 minutes. Remove the mold from the steamer and let cool, completely uncovered. Chill overnight or for 6 or more hours. To make into a Parm wedge, simply cut the square cheese in half diagonally for two wedges. Store in an airtight container for 7 to 10 days.

④ For best results, keep the cheese extra cold, if possible, and wait until just before you use it to pull it out of the fridge; otherwise, if the Parm sits out for longer than 30 minutes, it begins to get too soft to grate/shred.

cashew-free

gluten-free

soy-free

grain-free

Macadamia ASIAGO

makes one 12-ounce block

This is a cheese for those who like to indulge and savor, a cheese so indulgent that you may have a hard time convincing anyone that there is no dairy in sight. A smooth and buttery cheese like Asiago calls for a smooth and buttery replacement. Look no further because macadamia nuts have entered the chat. If you have a hard time finding macadamia nuts, cashews are a close second and will also work well for this! This is another cheese that shreds, slices, and melts beautifully. To shred this Asiago, pop it into the freezer for fifteen minutes right before grating, for best results.

THE GOODS

- 1 cup (125 g) macadamia nuts
- 1 tablespoon (5 g) nutritional yeast
- 1 teaspoon salt
- ⅓ cup (80 ml) refined coconut oil
- 1 teaspoon agar-agar
- 1 teaspoon sauerkraut juice
- 1 tablespoon (8 g) potato starch

THE METHOD

Combine the macadamia nuts, nutritional yeast, and salt in a *dry* high-powered blender. Blend on low speed for 30 seconds to create a crumble, and set aside. Combine the coconut oil, agar-agar, sauerkraut juice, and potato starch in a small saucepan, and whisk for about 4 minutes over low heat. If it starts to bubble over, lower the heat and keep stirring. After 4 minutes, add the hot coconut oil blend to the crumbled mixture in the blender, and blend again on low speed for about 60 seconds while using the accelerator stick, or until the entire mixture is well mixed. Pour into a silicone mold or a plastic wrap–lined glass container and refrigerate for 6 or more hours, or overnight. This will keep for 14 days in an airtight container in the fridge or for a month in the freezer.

cashew-free

gluten-free

soy-free

grain-free

hard

stinky

Creamy GORGONZOLA

makes one 6-inch round

If you like a stinky cheese, this one's for you. Gorgonzola is made by adding mold spores to milk fat and then waiting six to eight *months* before it's ready to eat—and even after all that waiting, Gorgonzola is too much for a lot of people. This Gorgonzola is easy to put together and you only have to wait 6 *hours* for the result. To get that stinky blue-and-green marble, I use spirulina, an algae that is rich in vitamins and minerals and can help protect your body from infection (it's also a way less weird replacement for mold spores). Spirulina is also the funky flavor, so if you like your Gorgonzola extra funky, add ⅛ teaspoon more of spirulina.

THE GOODS

- 1 (14-ounce [400 g]) block firm tofu
- 1 tablespoon (20 g) miso paste
- 1 tablespoon (15 ml) freshly squeezed lemon juice
- 1 teaspoon white wine vinegar
- 1 tablespoon (5 g) nutritional yeast
- 1¼ teaspoons salt
- ⅓ cup (80 ml) refined coconut oil, melted
- Pinch of spirulina powder

THE METHOD

Line a round 6-inch Glasslock container with cheesecloth (make sure the cheesecloth is big enough to later wrap over the top), then set aside. Combine the tofu, miso paste, lemon juice, white wine vinegar, nutritional yeast, and salt in a high-powered blender. Blend on medium speed for 60 seconds, or until well mixed. Add the melted coconut oil and blend for 30 seconds, or until everything is fully mixed. Pour the mixture into a clean bowl and carefully sprinkle the spirulina over the top, then gently fold the mixture two or three times into itself. Transfer to the prepared container and fold the cheesecloth over the top. Cap with a lid and refrigerate for 6 or more hours, or overnight. This will keep in the fridge for 5 to 6 days.

cashew-free

gluten-free

grain-free

MUENSTER

makes two 8-ounce blocks

Muenster is the underdog of the cheese world. While everyone is focused on Cheddar, or mozzarella, or Brie, a nutty, buttery, and mellow cheese like Muenster is the missing piece that often gets overlooked. It makes the most epic sub or the perfect picnic cheese board. The combination of blanched almonds, mustard powder, and lemon transforms these ingredients into a new kind of Muenster you might even love more than the original.

THE GOODS

1 to 2 teaspoons paprika
1½ cups (200 g) blanched almonds, soaked in hot water for 10 minutes, then drained
2 tablespoons (10 g) nutritional yeast
1 teaspoon salt
1 teaspoon mustard powder
½ teaspoon garlic powder
½ teaspoon onion powder
3 tablespoons (45 ml) freshly squeezed lemon juice
¾ cup (180 ml) Oat Hemp Milk (page 45)
1 tablespoon (10 g) agar-agar

THE METHOD

① Line a medium-size Glasslock container with cheesecloth (make sure the cheesecloth is big enough to later wrap over the top) and sprinkle the inner sides of the cloth with the paprika. Set aside.

② Combine the blanched almonds, nutritional yeast, salt, mustard powder, garlic powder, onion powder, and lemon juice in a high-powered blender (you'll need the accelerator stick) or food processor. Set aside. Combine the oat milk and agar-agar in a small saucepan, and whisk for 2 minutes over medium heat to dissolve the agar-agar. Add the mixture to the blender and blend until just combined. You will need to use the accelerator stick as you blend to get this one moving; it's thick. Scoop the mixture into the prepared container and fold the extra cheesecloth over the top. Let sit in the fridge for 4 to 6 hours before enjoying. After the cheese has set, remove from the fridge and from the cheesecloth, and sprinkle the edges with an extra dusting of paprika. Will keep for 7 days in the fridge.

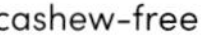
cashew-free

gluten-free

soy-free

oil-free

creamy

CHÈVRE LOG

makes two 10-ounce logs

I'd be lying if I said I never got drunk on a date and *accidentally* ate an entire log of goat cheese. It's safe to say that, as a single gal, the first date often wouldn't have stood a chance for a second, but you already know I kept coming back for my love affair with chèvre. This chèvre log is creamy, tangy, and freakishly like the real thing. It pairs perfectly with any grazing board, is a queen on a baguette, and absolutely slays for a first date. Macadamia nuts are the perfect base for this one as they add the perfect amount of decadence and creaminess. If you have an allergy, you can sub with cashews or blanched slivered almonds. No need to double this recipe for a date, as this makes two, so you can have one all to yourself.

THE GOODS

- 1 cup (130 g) macadamia nuts
- ½ cup (100 g) drained and crumbled firm tofu
- ¼ cup (60 ml) melted coconut oil, refined
- 1 tablespoon (5 g) nutritional yeast
- 1½ teaspoons salt
- 2 tablespoons (30 ml) freshly squeezed lemon juice
- 2 tablespoons (30 ml) sauerkraut juice
- 1 teaspoon miso paste
- 3 tablespoons (45 ml) No-Strain Almond Milk (page 42) or store-bought unsweetened plant-based milk of choice
- Optional: 2 tablespoons (6 g) dried herbs of your choice (I like basil, rosemary, and thyme)

THE METHOD

Combine all the ingredients in a high-powered blender and blend on high speed for 2 minutes, or until everything is fully smooth. You will have to use the blender's accelerator stick to get it moving and blend everything together. If you don't have an accelerator stick, use a food processor for this one! If you want to make logs, lay two 8 x 9-inch pieces of plastic wrap side by side on your work surface. Top each with a slightly smaller piece of cheesecloth. Dollop the mixture evenly onto each cheesecloth and then begin to wrap the cheesecloth and the plastic wrap around each portion of the mixture. To create a log shape, twist the sides opposite directions at the same time. Twist rubber bands around the sides and place the logs in a dish that will help keep their shape. For an easier mold option, line a Glasslock container with cheesecloth and carefully pour your mixture into the mold. Refrigerate for 6 hours to overnight before enjoying. If you want to have an herbed log, once the logs are set, roll them in 2 tablespoons (6 g) of mixed dried herbs. The logs keep well, in a sealed container, in the fridge for 7 to 10 days.

cashew-free

gluten-free

grain-free

Hot-Honey Peach BAKED BRIE

makes 14 ounces (1¾ cups)

Yee-haw! Hot honey (in this case, agave + sriracha) paired with ripe peaches and a baked Brie? Count me smitten. I could eat this every single day of my life if I had the chance. This recipe is perfect for summer evenings with a glass of sauvignon blanc or a lemonade. Fresh peaches are best, but frozen works great, too, especially if you need this when peaches aren't ripe or accessible near you. And, yes, I said "need" because this cheese is never a *want*, it's always a need.

THE GOODS

Brie:

- ½ cup (75 g) chopped yellow potatoes (if using Idaho, be sure to peel)
- 1 cup (140 g) blanched almonds, soaked in hot water for 15 minutes, then drained
- 1 tablespoon (20 g) miso paste
- 1 tablespoon (5 g) nutritional yeast
- 2 teaspoons salt
- 1 cup (240 ml) No-Strain Almond Milk (page 42) or store-bought unsweetened plant-based milk of choice
- ¼ cup (60 ml) unsweetened plain vegan yogurt
- 2 tablespoons (15 g) tapioca starch

Hot-Honey Peaches:

- 1 medium-size peach, pitted and diced
- 2 tablespoons (30 ml) agave nectar
- 1 tablespoon (15 ml) sriracha
- 1 teaspoon minced fresh rosemary

THE METHOD

① Preheat the oven to 400°F (205°C).

② Make the Brie: Combine all the Brie ingredients in a high-powered blender and blend on high speed for 1 to 2 minutes, or until fully mixed. Pour the mixture into a small saucepan over medium heat. Cook down for 6 to 7 minutes while stirring constantly with a rubber spatula. It will become thick and very cheesy-looking. Carefully, pour mixture into a 1-quart oven-safe dish and set aside.

③ Make the hot-honey peaches: Combine your peaches, agave, sriracha, and rosemary in a small bowl, and stir until the peaches are coated. Pour the coated peaches over the top of the Brie in an artful fashion, plopped straight on top of it. Cover and bake for 10 minutes, then bake for 5 minutes, uncovered. Serve immediately while warm with bread or toasties. Leftovers (as if) can be stored for 4 to 5 days in the fridge.

cashew-free

gluten-free

soy-free optional

oil-free

FETA

makes one 18-ounce block

If you're going to be salty about this breakup, then look no further because this household favorite is about to match your energy, big-time. We love a high-protein cheese, and this feta hits all the spots. With tofu as a base, this cheese stays super creamy and can easily be cubed to be popped into a brine or marinated in olive oil with herbs. Use this wherever you'd normally use feta and be sure to pair with olives, olive oil, and a really epic piece of pita bread.

THE GOODS

- 1 (14-ounce [400 g]) block firm tofu, drained and pressed (see pressing info on page 36)
- 1 tablespoon (20 g) miso paste
- 3 tablespoons (45 ml) freshly squeezed lemon juice
- 1 tablespoon (15 ml) white wine vinegar
- 1 tablespoon (15 ml) olive oil
- 2 tablespoons (5 g) nutritional yeast
- 2½ teaspoons salt
- ¾ cup (180 ml) water
- 2 tablespoons (20 g) agar-agar

THE METHOD

① Line a 6-inch container with cheesecloth, letting the cloth drape over the sides (you'll be folding it over later) and set aside.

② Combine all the ingredients, except the water and agar-agar, in a high-powered blender, and blend on medium speed for 30 to 60 seconds, or until you have a thick and smooth mixture. You may have to use an accelerator stick to get everything going. Keep this mixture nearby in the blender because you will need it ready to go quickly.

③ Combine your water and agar-agar in a small saucepan. Cook for 2 to 3 minutes over medium heat, stirring with a rubber spatula, just until it begins to thicken—it goes from 0 to 100 really fast. As soon as it starts to thicken, pour the agar-agar mixture straight into the blender. Blend everything together for 60 seconds, or until fully mixed. Pour the mixture into the prepared container. Fold the cheesecloth over the top and then top with a lid. Let sit in the refrigerator for at least 4 hours—for best results, let set overnight. Enjoy within 7 to 8 days.

nut-free

gluten-free

grain-free

oil-free

makes 10 ounces

I'm just going to say it: the incredible texture and versatility of this cheese makes this one the one you can't live without. It can be formed into a block of mozzarella, mozzarella balls, or large rounds of burrata cheese. It's the same base for all three with a different setting technique for each. With the mozzarella balls and burrata, you set them by scooping the hot cheese mixture into an ice bath. The longer the cheese sits in the ice bath, the firmer it will become. If you like a burrata that has a supersoft center, let it set for only three to four minutes in the ice bath. Use this cheese on the Neapolitan Vodka Caprese Pizza (page 249) and the Burrata Pesto Sando (page 181), to have your mind absolutely blown.

THE GOODS

- ¾ cup (120 g) cashews, soaked in hot water for 15 minutes, then drained
- 1¼ cups (300 ml) water
- ½ teaspoon salt
- 1 teaspoon nutritional yeast
- 1 teaspoon miso paste
- 1 tablespoon (10 g) agar-agar
- 2 tablespoons (15 g) tapioca starch

THE METHOD

Combine all the ingredients in a high-powered blender and blend on high speed until smooth, for about 1 minute. Pour the mixture into a saucepan and cook over medium-low heat for 6 to 7 minutes while stirring constantly with a rubber spatula. Once the mixture has turned thick and glossy, remove from the heat. Now it's time to pick whichever way you want to make your mozz.

Mozzarella Block: To make it into a block, pour the mozz into a 2-cup silicone mold or a plastic wrap–lined Glasslock container, cover, and chill in the fridge for 4 to 6 hours. Best enjoyed before 8 days.

grain-free

oil-free

Mozzarella Balls: Fill a large bowl with water and at least 3 cups (320 g) of ice. With a small spoon or small ice cream scooper, working one at a time, make 1-inch-diameter dollops or balls and drop them into the icy water. Dropping round mozzarella balls takes some jiggling and finesse, but you got this. It's easier to drop each ball on top of a layer of floating ice cubes. You should have seventeen to nineteen balls. Let the balls chill in the icy water for 15 minutes. Then transfer them to a jar and toss with salted water or olive oil. Balls will keep, refrigerated, for about a week.

Burrata: Fill a large bowl with water and at least 3 cups (320 g) of ice. With a large ice cream scooper, working one at a time, make 3-inch-diameter dollops or balls, and drop them into the icy water. Dropping round burrata balls takes some jiggling and finessing. It's easier to drop each ball on top of a layer of floating ice cubes. You should have six to eight burrata balls. Let the balls chill in the icy water for no more than 5 minutes. Best if served and enjoyed right away.

gluten-free

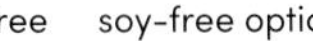
soy-free optional

grain-free

oil-free

LEFT TO RIGHT: Burrata, Mozzarella Balls, Mozzarella Block

MASCARPONE CHEESE

make 2½ cups

Mascarpone is for the indulgent and the lovers of curves. Mascarpone has double the fat content of a traditional cream cheese and is meant to be used on sweet dishes like cinnamon rolls and Danish, but it can also take a risotto to the next level. I used a combination of macadamia nuts and blanched almonds to pair the high fat with the creamy nuttiness they both provide. I absolutely love this "cheese" in the Tiramisu Espresso (page 257). I'm actually quite sure your mornings will never be the same after you try it!

THE GOODS

½ cup (70 g) macadamia nuts
½ cup (60 g) blanched almonds
½ cup (120 ml) unsweetened coconut yogurt
1 tablespoon (15 ml) freshly squeezed lemon juice
1½ tablespoons (22.5 ml) pure maple syrup
½ cup (120 ml) Coconut Milk (page 49), or full-fat canned

THE METHOD

Combine all the ingredients in a high-powered blender and blend on high speed for 1 to 2 minutes, or until everything is perfectly smooth. Pour into a Glasslock container and chill at least 4 hours before use. Keeps for 5 to 6 days in an airtight container in the fridge.

cashew-free

gluten-free

soy-free

oil-free

PANEER & PANELA & COTIJA

makes 2 cups

Because dairy-free cheese is becoming a plant culture of its own, I thought, *Why limit this to one vibe?* This cheese is high in protein and nutty yet also simple and can help elevate any dish, regardless of the culture. Think: a milky taste and a creamy yet slightly crumbly texture. It's actually so versatile that it can be used as a cheese replacement in sweet dishes as well. This cheese fits perfectly with the Paneer Masala (page 201), is the best addition to a torta, and can even be crumbled as a Cotija on top of chilaquiles.

THE GOODS

- 7 ounces (200 g) firm tofu, drained
- 1 cup (120 g) blanched almonds, soaked overnight or in hot water for 15 minutes, then drained
- 2 tablespoons (10 g) nutritional yeast
- 2 tablespoons (30 ml) apple cider vinegar
- 2 tablespoons (30 ml) freshly squeezed lemon juice
- 2 teaspoons salt (for Cotija, use 1 tablespoon instead)
- ¼ cup (60 ml) No-Strain Almond Milk (page 42) or unsweetened plant-based milk
- 1 tablespoon (10 g) agar-agar powder

THE METHOD

First up, make sure you have a medium-size Glasslock container or a silicone cheese mold ready to go because this process moves quickly! Combine all the ingredients, except the agar-agar, in a high-powered blender. Blend on high speed for 60 seconds until you have a smooth consistency. You might need to use the accelerator stick or scrape the sides with a spatula halfway through. Add the agar-agar and blend on high speed for 15 to 20 seconds. Transfer the mixture to a medium-size saucepan and cook over medium heat for 4 minutes while stirring constantly with a rubber spatula. You'll know it's done because the mixture will become superthick. Scoop this mixture into the container or mold, flatten the top, and either cover with a lid or press plastic wrap down so it's touching the top of the cheese. Refrigerate for 4 hours. This will keep for 7 to 8 days in the fridge.

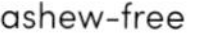
cashew-free

gluten-free

oil-free

5. Get SAUCED

A NECESSARY PART TO BREAKING UP is to get completely sauced, and luckily for us, in French cooking, the sauce is the boss. In so many cases, it is the delicious glue that holds everything together and can be one of the simplest ways to completely elevate your food. There is a massive misconception in the culinary world that, for a majority of traditional sauces to taste good, we need animal fat. And to that, I say . . . how boring! We're honoring where we came from by learning from it and finding a better way to do it. My dairy-free sauces are so much simpler, don't require whisking raw egg yolks or perfectly cooking butter with vinegar, and have the capability of seriously impressing your future in-laws. This chapter is filled with my versions of classics, such as hollandaise; it's also filled with sauces that will make your meal prep feel easy and joyful, and give you a sense of excitement when you eat. We're gettin' sauced, and we're doing it with plants.

Almost-Instant MANGO GREEK YOGURT

makes 2¼ cups

Some people wake up and blend smoothies; I wake up and blend this almost-instant Greek yogurt to put on my gigantic fruit bowls. This recipe was developed after a tired morning of opening my fridge and not finding much except a block of silken tofu. Turns out that adding some probiotic powder and a few more ingredients makes for a silky, protein-dense yogurt. I could take you through a long and risky process of fermentation for a yogurt, but who doesn't love to wake up and have a sure thing waiting for them in the morning? If you want this to thicken and ferment a bit like a regular yogurt, make it the night before and let it sit in the fridge overnight!

THE GOODS

- 8 ounces (225 g) silken tofu
- ½ cup (60 g) blanched almonds
- ¼ cup (60 ml) freshly squeezed lemon juice
- ½ cup (70 g) frozen mango (pineapple works too!)
- ½ teaspoon probiotic powder
- 1 tablespoon (15 ml) agave nectar

THE METHOD

Combine everything in a blender and blend until smooth, for about 30 seconds. You might need to use the accelerator stick if you have a Vitamix-style blender. Remove the lid, scrape down the sides with a rubber spatula, and blend for another 30 seconds. Enjoy immediately, or if you want a thicker yogurt, pour into a glass container with a lid and let set in the fridge for 3 hours or overnight, for the perfect consistency! Keeps for about 5 days in the fridge.

gluten-free

grain-free

oil-free

Spreadable BUTTER

makes 1½ cups

You need a relationship with someone who can do both: someone to be healthy with, and someone who will feed you baguettes. This recipe is that—in butter form. Not only is the base vegetables, but you can choose your emulsifier. If you want it thick like margarine, use refined coconut oil. If you want it smooth and fluffy, choose extra-virgin olive oil. Regardless of what you choose, this butter will perfectly brown a grilled cheese and will be the chef's kiss inside your mashed potatoes.

THE GOODS

1 cup (105 g) cauliflower florets
¼ cup (35 g) chopped carrot
¼ cup (60 ml) melted refined coconut oil or extra-virgin olive oil
½ teaspoon salt
1 teaspoon miso paste
¼ cup (40 g) cooked or canned great northern beans

THE METHOD

First up, set a large steamer basket above a few inches of water in a large, lidded pot, and bring to a boil over medium heat. Put in the cauliflower and carrot and steam until fork-tender, for about 10 minutes. Once the veggies are steamed, transfer them to a blender while they're still hot, along with the rest of the ingredients. Blend on a very low speed for 2 minutes; this will prevent splattering over the sides of the blender. Pour the mixture into a glass container with a lid, close it tightly, and let set for 4 hours in the fridge before enjoying. Store for 6 to 7 days in the fridge. Note that, because this is made with a base of veggies, you'll want to be sure to cook with this butter over low heat, as it browns quickly.

grain-free

The BUTTER BLOCK

makes 2 cups

Butter is truly one of the most universal and comforting ingredients out there, which is why so many people can't imagine a life without it. Butter is pure fat, which means that when it hits our taste buds, it literally makes us salivate, wanting more. In the food world, butter is pure lust. This is a refined version from my first cookbook; I had to add it here because you just can't break up with dairy without it. Use this butter *anywhere* a recipe calls for it. It's that lust you can't live without, made entirely from plants.

THE GOODS

1 cup (240 ml) melted refined coconut oil
¾ cup (180 ml) Whole Milk (page 46) or store-bought unsweetened cashew milk
½ teaspoon cider vinegar

Salted Butter:
All the above ingredients, plus 1 teaspoon salt

THE METHOD

Combine all the ingredients in a high-powered blender and blend on high speed for 60 seconds, or until fully smooth. Transfer to a Glasslock or airtight container, and let set in refrigerator for 6 hours to overnight. Store in the fridge for 5 to 7 days. When using it on bread or if you need it to spread, let it sit out on the counter for 10 to 15 minutes to soften up a bit before spreading.

HOLLANDAISE

makes 2½ cups

Hollandaise gave me a run for my money as a line cook and in culinary school. Whisking egg yolks with clarified butter over perfect heat *without* the sauce breaking over and over again is the true test of patience for a young cook. Fortunately, the method for this hollandaise is much easier than the classic French technique and it is the perfect dairy-free replacement. It's a recipe that will bring out your inner chef and give you an amazing sauce to serve on your home fries and biscuits the morning after.

THE GOODS

3 tablespoons (45 g) salted vegan butter (see the Butter Block, page 122)
3 garlic cloves, peeled and minced
3 tablespoons (35 g) cassava flour or oat flour
2¼ cups (540 ml) No-Strain Almond Milk (page 42) or store-bought unsweetened plant-based milk of choice
1 teaspoon Dijon mustard
2 teaspoons freshly squeezed lemon juice
½ teaspoon salt
1 tablespoon (5 g) nutritional yeast
¼ teaspoon ground white pepper
½ teaspoon ground turmeric

THE METHOD

Heat the vegan butter in a medium-size saucepan over medium-high heat until fully melted. Add the garlic and sauté for 30 seconds. Next up, using a rubber spatula, stir your cassava flour into the mixture, over medium-low to low heat, for 2 to 3 minutes. The mixture will become doughy and a little dry; don't worry, you're doing it right! Once it has turned a golden brown, add 2 cups (480 ml) of the milk, whisk to incorporate the cassava flour mixture into the milk, and then let simmer over low for 3 to 5 minutes to thicken. Next, toss in your Dijon, lemon juice, salt, nutritional yeast, white pepper, and turmeric, and keep whisking constantly over low heat for 4 to 6 more minutes. Remove from the heat, pour in the last ¼ cup (60 ml) of almond milk, and whisk. Set aside, covered with a lid. Pour on top of your favorite Benedict, or enjoy with Breakfast Pizza Pockets (page 211) or with home fries. Let cool completely before you store in an airtight container in the fridge. Best used within 5 days.

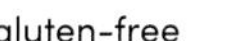

gluten-free soy-free grain-free

Barbie Béchamel

makes 4½ cups

In Barbie's dream house, every night is girls' night, and this sauce is the perfect addition. When you, or one of your friends, need a little extra empowerment or just want to feel like the queen you are, this sauce is sure to do just that. Beets are the perfect addition to this sauce. It's just enough to add a subtle sweetness and a gorgeous pop of color, without taking over the béchamel. You can put this sauce on pasta, or use it as a hollandaise replacement, or even throw it inside a lasagna. After all, in the world of Barbie, you make the rules.

THE GOODS

1 small (140 g) onion, peeled and sliced
1 cup (120 g) blanched slivered almonds
3 garlic cloves, peeled
1 small beet (150 g), peeled and diced
1 cup (240 ml) unsweetened plant-based milk
2 teaspoons miso paste
1 tablespoon (15 ml) freshly squeezed lemon juice
½ teaspoon salt
¼ teaspoon ground white pepper

If Making with Pasta:
1 pound (450 g) dried pasta (regular or gluten-free)
Lemon zest
¼ cup (30 g) chopped pistachios

THE METHOD

Set a large steamer basket above a few inches of water in a large, lidded pot. Bring to a boil over medium heat. Once hot, put in the onion, blanched almonds, garlic cloves, and beet, and steam until fork-tender, for about 10 minutes. When the veggies are soft, remove from the heat and transfer the contents of the steamer to a high-powered blender, along with the plant-based milk, miso paste, lemon juice, salt, and white pepper. Blend on high speed for 60 seconds, or until you have a beautiful pink sauce. Taste for garlic, salt, and pepper. Adjust, to taste. Set aside. If making ahead, store for 5 to 6 days in the fridge.

If making with pasta: Heat a large soup pot of salted water. Once the water is boiling, cook the pasta according to the package instructions. Drain your pasta when it is al dente, and place the drained pasta back in the empty soup pot along with the béchamel sauce. Reheat for 1 to 2 minutes over low heat, and then serve immediately with a garnish of lemon zest and chopped pistachios.

cashew-free

gluten-free optional

soy-free optional

oil-free

CREMA FOUR WAYS

makes 16 to 22 ounces (2 to 2½ cups)

This is the roundup of sauces that you want to put on *everything*. All the boxes you want checked in your must-have list are here. Allergy-friendly? Check. Creamy? Check. Versatile? Check. Works with any recipe? Check. Crazy delicious? Check, check, and check. For a plain sour cream or crema, stick to your base. For an epic sauce for potatoes or tacos or pasta or sandwiches, pick a flavor and have fun with it. Have a favorite herb or spice profile you don't see listed here? Add it to your base. Don't forget: it's your world and we're all just living in it.

STEP 1—PICK YOUR BASE

The Indulgent Queen:

2 cups (280 g) cashews, soaked in water overnight or in hot water for 15 minutes, then drained
1½ cups (360 ml) water
1 teaspoon salt
2 teaspoons white wine vinegar
2 tablespoons (30 ml) freshly squeezed lemon juice

The Protein Hero:

1 (14-ounce [400 g]) block firm tofu
2 tablespoons (30 ml) freshly squeezed lemon juice
1 tablespoon (5 g) nutritional yeast
1 tablespoon (15 ml) white wine vinegar
1 teaspoon salt
4 tablespoons (60 ml) unsweetened plant-based milk

STEP 2—PICK YOUR FLAVOR

Dill Poppy Seed:

¼ cup (15 g) minced fresh or (12 g) dried dill
2 tablespoons (30 ml) freshly squeezed lemon juice
1 teaspoon lemon zest
1 teaspoon poppy seeds
¼ teaspoon ground white pepper
½ teaspoon salt

Bai's Special Sauce:

1½ teaspoons to 1 tablespoon (7.5 to 15 ml) adobo sauce from a can of chipotle peppers
1½ teaspoons (7.5 ml) agave nectar
½ teaspoon garlic powder
½ teaspoon paprika
½ teaspoon onion powder
½ teaspoon salt
1 tablespoon (15 ml) freshly squeezed lemon juice

THE METHOD

Pick your base, then combine all its ingredients in a high-speed blender and blend on medium speed for 60 seconds, or until smooth and creamy. If you're adding a flavor, add its ingredients once the base is blended. Blend again for 30 seconds and store in a squeeze bottle or a mason jar in the fridge. Will keep for about 7 days.

nut-free optional

gluten-free

soy-free optional

grain-free

oil-free

Guajillo Sauce

makes 40 ounces

Oof. This creamy guajillo sauce is the stuff dreams are made of. A little spicy, a little sweet, a little complex, and so dang delicious. It's good enough to use on its own as a salsa for chips, or it can take the Chiles Rellenos (page 179) to the next level. At least once a month this sauce lands in my meal prep rotation because it's so easy to make a delicious meal with this as the vessel. Wondering where to get the chilies? You can easily get a large bag of the dried guajillos at your local Mexican market or online.

The Goods

- 1 teaspoon olive oil
- 2 dried guajillo peppers, roughly chopped
- 1 onion, peeled and diced small
- 1 teaspoon salt
- 4 garlic cloves, peeled and sliced
- 1 teaspoon ground coriander
- 1 teaspoon smoked paprika
- ½ teaspoon ground cinnamon
- 1 red bell pepper, seeded and sliced
- 3 cups (720 ml) veggie broth
- ½ cup (80 g) almonds
- 4 large pitted Medjool dates, small chopped
- ½ cup (120 ml) unsweetened plant-based milk

The Method

① Combine the olive oil and dried peppers in a 3-quart saucepan over medium heat. Sauté, stirring, for about 20 seconds to soften up the peppers and release their aromas. Add the onion and ½ teaspoon of the salt, and let cook, stirring, for about 2 minutes, or until the onion becomes soft, fragrant, and translucent. Add the garlic, coriander, smoked paprika, and cinnamon, and let the spices toast for about 15 seconds. Add the bell pepper and sauté for about 1 minute. If the spices are starting to burn against the surface of the pan, add 1 tablespoon (15 ml) of the veggie broth to deglaze. Add the almonds and dates, and sauté for 1 minute more. Pour in the veggie broth, stir, cover, and cook over low heat for 15 minutes.

② Then transfer the sauce to a high-powered blender, along with the plant-based milk and the remaining ½ teaspoon of salt. Blend on medium speed for about 1 minute, then taste for desired salt. Serve with tacos, enchiladas, or Chiles Rellenos (page 179). Will keep for 7 to 9 days in the fridge.

cashew-free

gluten-free

soy-free

NACHO CHEESE with Mush-riso

makes 48 ounces (6 cups)

There are about a million recipes for a vegan nacho cheese, but few remain neutral in the world of food allergies. I wanted to create a recipe that would be good for the kids after school, the spouses on game day, and for the girlies with their cravings. A recipe *anyone* can eat regardless of their food allergies. This nacho cheese brings out the best in the veggie world and—bonus—has a chorizo made of mushrooms folded inside. It's the easiest way to get picky eaters to snack on veggies, and it's the absolute best served over crispy potatoes or smothered over a burrito.

THE GOODS

Nacho Cheese Sauce:

- 1 small onion, peeled and sliced
- 3 garlic cloves, peeled
- 1 jalapeño, seeds and stem removed (optional)
- 1 orange bell pepper, seeds and stem removed
- 2 medium-size carrots, chopped
- 2 medium-size yellow potatoes, chopped
- 1 teaspoon salt
- 1 cup (240 ml) Oat Hemp Milk (page 45) or store-bought unsweetened plant-based milk of choice
- ¼ cup (30 g) hemp seeds
- ½ teaspoon ground turmeric
- 1 tablespoon (5 g) nutritional yeast

The Mush-riso:

- 2 cups (130 g) chopped cremini mushrooms
- 2 cups (110 g) chopped shiitake mushrooms
- 1 teaspoon salt
- 1 teaspoon avocado oil
- 2 teaspoons chili powder
- 1 teaspoon garlic powder
- 1 teaspoon onion powder
- 1 teaspoon ground cumin
- 1 teaspoon ground coriander
- 1 teaspoon paprika
- ½ teaspoon chipotle powder
- 1 teaspoon agave nectar

THE METHOD

① ***Begin the nacho cheese sauce:*** Set a medium-size steamer basket above a few inches of water in a large, lidded pot. Bring to a simmer over medium-low heat, then put in the onion, garlic, jalapeño, bell pepper, carrots, and potatoes. Cover the pot and let steam for 10 to 15 minutes, or until the veggies are fork-tender. Remove and set aside the steamed veggies when they are done.

recipe continues →

nut-free

gluten-free

soy-free

grain-free optional

oil-free

② ***Meanwhile, make the mush-riso:*** Place a large sauté pan over medium-high heat. Combine the mushrooms and salt in the pan, then dry sauté for about 2 minutes to release the water from the mushrooms. Essentially, to dry sauté means that you don't use any oil or broth to cook these, letting the natural oils and water of the mushrooms do the work here. You can also press down with a wooden spoon to help release the water as you are cooking. Add the avocado oil and all the rest of the mush-riso ingredients, except the agave, and sauté for 2 to 3 minutes, or until golden brown. For the last 30 seconds of sautéing, add the agave to caramelize the mushrooms. Remove from the heat and set aside.

③ ***Back to the cheese sauce:*** Combine the steamed veggies and the rest of the cheese ingredients in a high-powered blender. Blend on high speed until smooth and well mixed, for about 1 minute. Remove the lid and fold the mushrooms into the cheese sauce. Pour over nachos or potatoes, use on sandwiches or tacos, or smother a burrito. Leftovers (as if) will last in the fridge for 4 to 5 days.

④ ***How to make this queso fundido:*** Pour the finished mixture into an oven-safe dish (I love to use a small cast-iron pan) and broil at 500°F (260°C) for 3 to 4 minutes, or until browning on top and bubbling. Serve with fresh tortillas or tortilla chips.

nut-free

gluten-free

soy-free

grain-free optional

oil-free

VODKA SAUCE with Rigatoni

serves 3 or 4

Sometimes, all you need to mend a broken heart is a gigantic bowl of pasta drowning in vodka sauce, all to yourself. It doesn't hurt if it's loaded with Potato Parmesan (page 95). Carbs have truly gotten me over some of the worst breakups of my life, and the breakup with dairy is no exception. You can't use just any plant-based milk replacement here. I made the Whole Milk (page 46) with this recipe in mind. You need a thick, luscious, and creamy milk to do the job here. This sauce is best finished with pasta water. So grab a box of rigatoni, a bottle of wine, and a girlfriend, and have a night just for the girls—and for the carbs.

THE GOODS

- 1 pound (450 g) dried rigatoni pasta or whatever other pasta you have on hand
- 1 teaspoon salt, plus a generous pinch for pasta water
- 1 teaspoon olive oil
- 1 shallot, minced
- 4 garlic cloves, minced
- 3 tablespoons (40 g) tomato paste
- ½ teaspoon ground white pepper
- 1 cup (240 ml) vodka
- 1 batch Whole Milk (page 46), or for nut-free, use 1 batch Protein Hero Crema (page 129)
- Potato Parmesan (page 95), fresh basil leaves, and freshly ground black pepper, for garnish

THE METHOD

① First up, boil your water for your pasta in a large soup pot. Add the generous pinch of salt. You want it salty like the sea to yield the best pasta! Cook the pasta according to the package directions for al dente, drain, and remember to save 1 cup (240 ml) of the pasta water for the sauce. If cooking gluten-free pasta, rinse the noodles in cold water to prevent them from getting mushy.

recipe continues →

gluten-free optional

soy-free

grain-free optional

② Meanwhile, for the vodka sauce, heat the olive oil in a large, deep sauté pan over medium heat. Once hot, add the shallot and garlic, and sauté for about 30 seconds, or until they start to turn golden brown. Add the tomato paste and teaspoon of salt. Stir well with a wooden or silicone spatula so that the shallot and garlic become coated with the tomato paste. You want this to cook for about 90 seconds, or until you get a golden layer of cooked tomato paste at the bottom of the mixture. Add the white pepper and vodka, and let simmer on medium-low heat until the liquid is reduced by half, in 5 to 7 minutes. Add the whole milk to the pan, stir well, cover with a lid, and cook for 7 to 10 minutes, or until the mixture thickens and becomes silky smooth. Finally, add the reserved pasta water, stir well, and taste for salt preference.

③ Once the sauce is seasoned to your liking, turn off the heat, add the cooked pasta, and toss with the sauce so everything is coated. Transfer your preferred amounts to individual serving bowls. Top with grated Parm, basil leaves, and black pepper. If making this ahead of time, store the sauce in an airtight mason jar in the fridge for about a week.

gluten-free optional

soy-free

grain-free optional

Baked TRUFFLE MAC

serves 3 or 4

If you think no dairy means no mac and cheese, I'm just going to say it: you're wrong. And because I'm always extra, I had to make this a white truffle mac—bonus points if you bake it with the breadcrumbs and truffle salt. A truffle mac this good can help anyone see that life on the other side of dairy is a life worth living after all.

THE GOODS

- 1 onion, peeled and large chopped
- 2 medium-size white carrots, large chopped
- 2 small yellow potatoes, large chopped
- 4 garlic cloves, peeled
- 1½ teaspoons salt
- ½ cup (30 g) hemp seeds
- 2 tablespoons (15 g) nutritional yeast
- ½ teaspoon ground white pepper
- 2 tablespoons (20 g) tapioca or arrowroot starch
- 2 cups (480 ml) No-Strain Almond Milk (page 42) or store-bought unsweetened plant-based milk of choice
- 1 tablespoon (15 ml) white truffle oil (2 tablespoons if you're feelin' frisky)
- 16 ounces (450 g) dried elbow noodles (GF if needed), cooked per package instructions

To Bake:

- 1 cup (150 g) vegan breadcrumbs (GF if needed)
- 1 tablespoon (2 g) herbes de Provence
- 1 teaspoon granulated garlic
- ½ teaspoon freshly ground black pepper
- ½ teaspoon salt (or truffle salt to add more pizzazz)
- 3 tablespoons (45 ml) olive oil

THE METHOD

No-Bake Method: Combine the onion, white carrots, potatoes, garlic, and 1 teaspoon of the salt in a small, lidded soup pot. Cover with water, put on the lid, and cook over medium heat for 15 minutes, or until fork-tender. Drain the cooked veggies through a colander and transfer them to a high-powered blender, along with the hemp seeds, nutritional yeast, white pepper, tapioca starch, almond milk, and truffle oil, and blend on medium-high speed for 45 seconds, or until the mixture is super creamy and smooth. Pour the mixture into a saucepan and cook over medium-low heat, stirring with

recipe continues →

nut-free

gluten-free optional

soy-free

a rubber spatula every 30 seconds or so, for 5 minutes. Remove from the heat and immediately serve with the cooked noodles, or refrigerate for later in a mason jar for an amazing pizza (page 249). You can also meal prep the sauce ahead of time, as it keeps for 5 to 6 days in the fridge.

Bake Method: Do everything for the no-bake method except for reheating the sauce. Preheat the oven to 350°F (177°C). Combine the sauce and cooked pasta in a bowl, then pour the saucy noodles into a 9 x 13-inch baking dish. In a small bowl, combine all the ingredients for the breadcrumb topping. Top the mac and cheese with the breadcrumb topping and bake for 20 minutes. Enjoy immediately! Keep in mind that gluten-free noodles will keep for only about a day for leftovers; regular noodles will keep for 3 to 4 days.

nut-free

gluten-free optional

soy-free

Home-Style GRAVY

serves 4

Imagine a brunch where you went to town on Grandma's country gravy with a Bloody Mary and instead of feeling horrible, stuffed with regret afterward, you felt amazing and ready to take on the day. This isn't just a fairy tale; this is my ultimate country gravy. It will convince even the most southern of folks that it was made with an old family recipe. I made this GF by using cassava flour, and swapped in ground walnuts for the low-grade ground beef. Not only will your biscuits (or potatoes) be happy as ever in this sauce, but your gut will thank you for it too.

THE GOODS

3 tablespoons (45 ml) olive oil
1 small white onion, peeled and minced
1 to 1½ teaspoons (6 to 9 g) salt
4 garlic cloves, peeled and minced
¼ cup (45 g) cassava flour
4 cups (960 ml) No-Strain Almond Milk (page 42), or for nut-free, use Oat Hemp Milk (page 45)
½ to 1 teaspoon ground white pepper
¼ cup (10 g) chopped fresh parsley
½ cup (50 g) ground walnuts (optional), or for nut-free, use steamed lentils
1 cup (240 ml) water (optional)

THE METHOD

① Combine the olive oil, onion, and 1 teaspoon of the salt in a large saucepan over medium heat. Cook, stirring with a wooden spoon, for about 7 minutes, or until the onion is fragrant and translucent. Add the garlic and cook for 1 minute more. Add the cassava flour and stir for about 10 seconds to get everything coated with the flour. Add the almond milk, then lower the heat to medium-low and stir well. The mixture will start to thicken; keep stirring and cook for about 10 more minutes. Add the white pepper, ¼ teaspoon at a time—if you're sensitive to pepper, add about ½ teaspoon total; if you like a kick, add 1 teaspoon! After the 10 minutes, add the parsley and walnuts for some color and texture. Stir and cook for another 1 to 2 minutes. At this point, if you want it thick, keep it the way it is; if you want it a bit smoother and thin, add the water, ¼ cup (60 ml) at a time, until you get the perfect consistency for you.

② Serve this delicious gravy with mashed potatoes, biscuits, or fried tofu. Store the gravy for 6 to 7 days in the fridge.

nut-free optional

gluten-free

soy-free

makes 16 ounces (2 cups)

Whether you're eating this with some vegan chicken nuggets for the ultimate girl dinner or making this with the Crab Potato Pancakes (page 239) for the holidays, this tartar sauce is such an easy way to up-level any meal. It's completely allergy-friendly, with barely any prep required. Easy to make, delicious, and a perfect match for everyone? Count me in.

THE GOODS

1 cup (140 g) hulled sunflower seeds, soaked in hot water for 15 minutes, then drained
½ teaspoon salt, plus more if needed
2 teaspoons white wine vinegar
2 teaspoons Dijon mustard
2 heaping teaspoons capers
1 teaspoon agave nectar
¼ cup (60 ml) freshly squeezed lemon juice
¾ cup (180 ml) water
½ cup (120 ml) unsweetened plant-based milk
3 tablespoons (5 g) minced fresh chives

THE METHOD

Combine all the ingredients, except the chives, in a high-powered blender. Blend on medium speed for 60 seconds, or until smooth. Add the chives and pulse eight to ten times or until evenly incorporated. Keep chilled in an airtight container or mason jar. Use within 5 to 6 days.

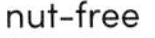

gluten-free

soy-free

grain-free

oil-free

IT'S NOTHING PERSONAL,
IT'S VIBRATIONAL

6. MAIN MEALS Worthy of a Third Date

THIS CHAPTER IS DEDICATED to not only the meals that get us through any rough breakup but also the gateway recipes that can start something new. These are the recipes that are *so* delicious they're only acceptable to make for someone if they've made it to the third date. This collection was inspired by my love to wine and dine, paired with my deep frustration for the lack of amazing dairy-free options while doing so. We're going for that comforting, creamy, savory, and sometimes umami magic that'll make you think "I got this" in this new phase of your life. You'll find breakfast recipes like Passion Fruit French Toast. You'll impress yourself with the Chiles Rellenos and the Creamy Black Garlic Ramen. And most important, you'll bring the heat to any third date with the One-Pot Meyer Lemon Cacio e Pepe and the Birria Tacos.

Raspberry Horchata FLUFFY PANCAKES

makes 8 to 10 pancakes

Truly thriving, in my eyes, is waking up in a crazy comfortable bed with linen sheets, ordering room service, and these fluffy pancakes are what greet you at the door. This recipe will easily climb to number one on your roster and be the go-to pancake that will immediately transport you to brunch bliss. It's got very few easy-to-find ingredients paired with the Raspberry Horchata (page 62), making this an absolute must-make regardless of whether or not you're gluten-free.

THE GOODS

- 1½ cups (225 g) 1-to-1 gluten-free baking flour
- 1 tablespoon (15 g) baking powder
- 1 tablespoon (10 g) coconut sugar (sub organic cane sugar for coconut allergy)
- ½ teaspoon salt
- 1¾ cups (420 ml) Raspberry Horchata (page 62)
- ¼ cup (60 ml) melted salted vegan butter (see the Butter Block, page 122)
- 1½ cups (180 g) raspberries, for garnish
- Pure maple syrup, for serving

THE METHOD

Combine your 1-to-1 baking flour, baking powder, coconut sugar, and salt in a large bowl, and mix with a fork until everything is fully incorporated. Now, pour in your raspberry horchata and 2 tablespoons (30 ml) of the melted vegan butter, and mix until you have a batter. Be careful not to overmix; stir just until everything is combined. Set aside. Heat 1½ teaspoons of the remaining melted vegan butter in a large nonstick skillet over medium heat. Once the butter is melted, add ¼ cup (60 ml) of batter for each pancake and lower the heat to low. Cook for about 90 seconds per each side. The cooking time will depend on burner size and the thickness of your pan. You want the bottom to be perfectly golden brown before flipping. Repeat for each batch with your remaining vegan butter until all the batter is cooked. If serving for a crowd, you can place the finished pancakes on a baking sheet and store in the oven at 170°F (77°C) to keep them warm, or just serve and enjoy each batch immediately. Garnish with raspberries and drizzle with maple syrup.

Strawberry Cheesecake CREAM CHEESE DANISH

makes 18 small Danishes

There's nothing much better than a fresh batch of pastries baking in your oven. You don't need to be a pastry chef for these either. Instead of going through the process of making your own pastry dough, all you have to do is head to the freezer section of your grocery store and buy some vegan puff pastry. The Strawberry Cheesecake Cream Cheese (page 84) is more than ideal for these little bites of heaven, and the second these come out of the oven, you'll be thinking you could maybe even start a second career as a pastry chef, after all. Be sure to eat these right away, as they're meant to be enjoyed immediately.

THE GOODS

- 1 (17.5-ounce [490 g]) package vegan puff pastry
- Strawberry Cheesecake Cream Cheese (page 84)
- 10 fresh strawberries, hulled and chopped
- ½ cup (120 ml) unsweetened plant-based milk
- 1 tablespoon (12 g) coconut sugar (sub organic cane sugar for coconut allergy)
- ⅓ cup + 2 tablespoons (60 g) powdered sugar

THE METHOD

① Thaw out and unroll two sheets of puff pastry dough onto a large, flat surface. Once the puff pastry is 80 percent thawed out, preheat the oven to 400°F (205°C). Unroll and cut each puff pastry sheet into nine squares by cutting in thirds one way, then again into thirds going the other way; you will have a total of eighteen squares. Working one square at a time, place about 1 tablespoon (15 g) of the strawberry cream cheese onto each square. Top with a few pieces of the fresh strawberries, reserving the remaining berries for garnish. You can keep them square as they are or fold a pair of corners over the center to overlap. Place the finished pastries on a large, parchment paper–lined baking sheet.

soy-free optional

② Once all the pastry squares are filled with cream cheese, pour half the plant-based milk into a small bowl to use as a milk wash. With a pastry brush, brush any exposed areas of pastry with the milk wash, and then sprinkle coconut sugar over those areas. Once you have sprinkled them with coconut sugar, bake them for 15 minutes, or until golden brown.

③ ***While they bake, make the icing:*** In a separate small bowl, combine your powdered sugar with the remaining half of the plant-based milk, and whisk together until you have a smooth frosting. Set aside.

④ When the Danishes are golden brown, remove them from the oven and then, using a spoon, drizzle a generous amount of icing over the hot pastries. Let cool for 5 minutes, then serve with a garnish of fresh strawberries.

soy-free optional

Passion Fruit FRENCH TOAST

makes 8 to 10 slices of toast; serves 3 or 4

This is the best French toast to make for your girlfriends or family, but if you want a sweet breakfast for two, save half the batter and have French toast all weekend long! French toast is often one of those brunch items you can rarely ever find dairy-free, and I'm here to change that. Coconut milk is used because of its fat content, yielding a deliciously golden-brown crust. When the toast is paired with a passion fruit coulis, macadamia nuts, and mascarpone cheese, you'll feel that you've been transported to a tropical island resort straight from your kitchen. Why go out for brunch when you can have it this good at home?

THE GOODS

Passion Fruit Coulis:

- 2 cups (280 g) fresh or frozen passion fruit
- ⅓ cup (80 ml) agave nectar

French Toast:

- 1 cup (240 ml) Coconut Milk (page 49), or canned
- 7 ounces (200 g) silken tofu
- ½ teaspoon ground cinnamon
- 2 tablespoons (25 g) coconut sugar
- 1 teaspoon pure vanilla extract
- 2 tablespoons (30 ml) melted salted butter (from the Butter Block, page 122), plus more for frying
- 4 or 5 thick slices day-old vegan sourdough or GF bread, cut in half

For Garnish:

- Mascarpone Cheese (page 113)
- Handful of macadamia nuts, minced
- Ground cinnamon

THE METHOD

① *Make the coulis:* Combine the passion fruit and agave nectar in a small sauté pan, cook over medium heat for 2 minutes, then continue to cook on medium-low, stirring occasionally, for 10 minutes. The consistency will be smooth and a little runny; it will stick to your spoon like maple syrup but won't be thick like honey. Remove from the heat and let it cool.

recipe continues →

gluten-free optional

Passion Fruit French Toast, continued

② *Make the French toast:* Combine the coconut milk, silken tofu, cinnamon, coconut sugar, vanilla, and 2 tablespoons (30 ml) of the melted butter in a large high-powered blender, and blend on high speed for 60 seconds, or until fully smooth. Pour your mixture into a large bowl with a flat bottom. Set aside.

③ Heat a nonstick skillet or crepe pan over medium-low heat, and add 1 teaspoon of butter. Dip a slice of your bread into the batter, let it soak in for a few seconds on each side, then place the soaked slice on the hot pan. Once you lay it down on the skillet, try not to move it too much; this will help get that golden crust. Cook each side for 5 to 6 minutes for the first batch, and then 4 to 5 minutes for the later ones. Once each side is golden brown, transfer the toast from the pan onto a serving plate. Serve immediately while still hot. Garnish with a scoop or two of mascarpone cheese, macadamia nuts, and a sprinkle of cinnamon.

gluten-free optional

The Grilled Wedge with BLUE CHEESE DRESSING

makes 4 salads

Hot-girl summer called and it wants all this salad has to offer. I love a wedge, but I'm bothered by the carbon-copy wedge salad you see everywhere. Our summers need a little individuality, and this salad is the perfect fit. This grilled wedge is complete with shishito peppers, zucchini, grilled avocado, and a blue "cheese" dressing that'll have you serving this at all your summer cookouts from here on out.

THE GOODS

Coconut Bacon:

2 cups (240 g) coconut chips
2 tablespoons (30 ml) liquid aminos
2 tablespoons (30 ml) pure maple syrup
1 tablespoon (15 ml) liquid smoke
1 teaspoon paprika

Salad:

1 teaspoon olive oil (optional), for grilling
1 medium-size zucchini, thickly sliced
2 avocados, pitted, quartered, and peeled
7 or 8 shishito peppers
½ teaspoon granulated garlic
½ teaspoon salt
1 head iceberg lettuce, quartered
1 cup (140 g) cherry tomatoes, halved

Dressing:

1 batch Indulgent Queen Crema (page 129)
½ cup (120 ml) unsweetened plain plant-based yogurt
3 tablespoons (60 g) miso paste
2 tablespoons (10 g) nutritional yeast
1 tablespoon (15 ml) agave nectar
1 teaspoon salt
1 teaspoon mustard powder
½ teaspoon freshly ground black pepper
1 tablespoon (15 ml) cider vinegar
1 tablespoon (15 ml) freshly squeezed lemon juice
¼ teaspoon spirulina powder

THE METHOD

① *Make the coconut bacon:* Combine all its ingredients in a bowl, then stir until everything is fully mixed. Let marinate for 15 or more minutes. Afterward, line a baking sheet with

recipe continues →

gluten-free

grain-free

oil-free optional

parchment paper and pour your bacon onto it. Spread the bacon slices flat, evenly across the pan, slightly spaced apart from one another. Bake for 6 to 7 minutes. Shake them up, then bake for 3 more minutes (9 to 10 minutes total) until they're evenly browned. Remove from the oven. As the coconut bacon cools off, it will become crispy and hard. Set aside.

② *Next, make the salad:* Preheat the oven to 325°F (163°C). Heat the olive oil on a grill or grill pan to medium-high heat. If making this oil-free, make sure to use a nonstick grill pan. Place all the zucchini, avocado quarters, and shishitos in a single layer on the pan and grill each side, sprinkling them with the granulated garlic and salt, for 3 to 5 minutes, or until they have golden-brown marks. Remove from the heat and set aside.

③ *Now, make the dressing:* Combine all the dressing ingredients in a high-powered blender and blend on high speed for 45 to 60 seconds. Set aside.

④ To serve, cut each quarter of the iceberg lettuce into two or three wedges, divide the wedges among four individual serving plates, then garnish with cherry tomatoes, coconut bacon, and a few spoonfuls of the cooked zucchini, avocado, and shishitos. Drizzle a generous amount of the dressing over the top and enjoy immediately. The dressing will stay fresh in the fridge for about 5 days, and the bacon is best enjoyed within 2 days. You can re-crisp the bacon in your toaster oven at 400°F (205°C) for a few minutes.

gluten-free

grain-free

oil-free optional

Broccoli CHEDDAR SOUP

serves 4 or 5

The kiddos need love, too, and this classic is for them and for your child within. This Broccoli Cheddar Soup is somewhat of an initiation to cooking dairy-free. You think that there's no way you can make veggies taste like cheesy Cheddar goodness, but once you try it, it's like a whole new world opens up. It's a hug in a bowl. It's an easy way to sneak in veggies. And most important, it pairs perfectly with grilled cheese.

THE GOODS

4 cups (960 ml) veggie broth, plus 1 tablespoon (15 ml) for cooking vegetables
1 onion, medium diced
1 small leek, rinsed and sliced
1½ teaspoons salt
2 celery ribs, sliced
3 medium-size white carrots, medium diced
2 small yellow potatoes, medium diced
3 garlic cloves, peeled and sliced
1 tablespoon (20 g) white miso paste
½ cup (70 g) cashews or (65 g) hemp seeds
½ teaspoon freshly ground black pepper
1½ cups (360 ml) Coconut Milk (page 49) or 1 (14-ounce [400-ml]) can, or 1½ cups (360 ml) Oat Hemp Milk (page 45)
1 tablespoon (5 g) nutritional yeast
1 teaspoon ground turmeric
3 cups (195 g) shaved broccoli tops
1 teaspoon freshly squeezed lemon juice

THE METHOD

① Heat the tablespoon (15 ml) of veggie broth in a large soup pot over medium-high heat. Once your pot is hot, add the onion, leek, and salt. Sauté for 2 to 3 minutes, or until the onion and leek are soft and fragrant. Toss in your celery, white carrots, and potatoes, and sauté for 3 to 5 minutes over medium-high heat. If you find that they are browning too quickly, add a few tablespoons (about 30 ml) of the remaining veggie broth to deglaze the pan. As your veggies turn golden brown, add the garlic,

recipe continues →

nut-free optional

gluten-free

soy-free optional

oil-free

miso paste, cashews, and pepper, and sauté for another 2 to 3 minutes. Add the 4 cups (960 ml) of veggie broth and coconut milk, cover with a lid, and cook over medium-low heat for 15 to 20 minutes.

2 By now, the carrots, potatoes, and cashews should be fork-tender. Transfer the hot soup to a large, heat-resistant high-powered blender (or leave in the pot and use an immersion blender), and blend on high speed until you have a smooth, pureed soup. If done in a high-powered blender, transfer back into the soup pot with the heat turned off, and toss in the nutritional yeast, turmeric, shaved broccoli, and lemon juice. Mix well. Let sit for 3 to 5 minutes with the lid on, which will allow the hot soup to cook the shaved broccoli. Taste for desired salt and serve with a grilled (vegan) cheese sandwich! Stores well in the fridge for 6 to 7 days or in the freezer. If freezing, make sure to leave some room for the soup to expand in the container.

nut-free optional

gluten-free

soy-free optional

oil-free

French Onion FUNGI SOUP

serves 4

French onion soup is the epitome of taking things slow and savoring the moment. This version is made completely from plants, as we let the cows just be cows here by using veggie broth and the epically versatile pourable mozzarella. The addition of mixed mushrooms not only elevates this dish but also adds a superfood punch by incorporating gut- and immune-boosting properties that will leave you feeling like the baddie you are. Use whatever mushrooms you can get your hands on and be sure to savor the slow moments of caramelizing onions and watching the pourable mozzarella become *magic* under the broiler.

THE GOODS

- 2 tablespoons (30 ml) olive oil or veggie broth (if oil-free)
- 6 medium-size yellow onions, peeled and sliced
- 1½ teaspoons salt
- 1 tablespoon (3 g) dried thyme
- ½ teaspoon freshly ground black pepper
- 1 tablespoon (15 ml) vegan Worcestershire sauce
- 1 tablespoon (15 ml) agave nectar
- 4 cups (960 ml) veggie broth
- 4 garlic cloves, peeled and sliced
- 16 ounces (450 g) mixed mushrooms, sliced (cremini, oyster, shiitake)
- 8 thick baguette slices (GF if needed)
- Pourable Mozzarella (page 88)

THE METHOD

① Heat a 5-quart stockpot over medium heat. Once hot, put in the olive oil, the onion, and 1 teaspoon of the salt. Sauté for 15 minutes to cook down the onions. After 15 minutes, add the thyme, pepper, Worcestershire sauce, and agave nectar. Stir and cook for another 10 minutes. Use a splash of veggie broth to deglaze from time to time, if the onions start to burn against

recipe continues →

nut-free optional

gluten-free optional

soy-free

oil-free optional

the surface of the pan. Add the garlic and cook, occasionally stirring, for another 10 minutes, to get the garlic fragrant and golden brown. Add the mushrooms and sauté for 10 more minutes to cook down. Pour in the veggie broth and the remaining ½ teaspoon of salt, and cook on medium-low, covered, for 10 to 15 minutes.

② Taste for salt, then remove from the heat. Preheat the broiler to 450°F (232°C). Divide the soup among four oven-safe soup bowls, filling each about three-quarters full. Top each with two slices of your baguette and a generous pouring of mozzarella. Set the soup bowls on a baking sheet to make transporting them to and from the oven a bit easier. Place the bowls, on their pan, on the top rack of the oven and broil for 3 to 6 minutes, depending on your oven. Keep an eye on them and cook until each top is golden brown. Enjoy immediately while hot. You can make the broth up to 3 days ahead of time and freeze if you have a lot left over. Be sure to leave some room in the container for the soup to expand if you do freeze it.

nut-free optional

gluten-free optional

soy-free

oil-free optional

Smoked Maitake DUMPLING SOUP

serves 4 or 5

Nothing hits the spot on a chilly day quite like steamed dumplings within a savory soup. These dumplings are perfectly fluffy and a little smoky, which makes for the best pairing with the maitake and butternut squash soup. Maitake mushrooms are such an incredible meat replacement because they take on a meat-like texture while giving the dish an immune-boosting superpower and a huge serving of vitamin D. The dumplings are so easy to make, already GF, and you can cut them into whatever shape your heart desires. It's a soup-er recipe that you'll come back to year after year!

THE GOODS

- 1 tablespoon (15 ml) olive oil
- 1 onion, peeled and small diced
- 1 teaspoon salt
- 2 medium-size carrots, small diced
- 2 celery ribs, small diced
- 3 garlic cloves, peeled and minced
- 1 small butternut squash, peeled, seeded, and medium diced
- 1 tablespoon (3 g) chopped fresh oregano
- 1 tablespoon (3 g) chopped fresh rosemary
- 16 ounces (450 g) maitake mushrooms
- ½ teaspoon ground white pepper
- 8 cups (1.9 L) veggie broth

Dumplings:

- 2 cups (300 g) 1-to-1 gluten-free baking flour blend or all-purpose flour
- 4 teaspoons baking powder
- 1 teaspoon salt
- 1 teaspoon smoked paprika
- 4 tablespoons (60 g) cold salted butter (see the Butter Block, page 122)
- ¾ cup (180 ml) unsweetened plant-based milk (oat, almond, soy, or cashew)

THE METHOD

① Heat the olive oil in a large soup pot over medium heat. Once hot, add the onion and salt and sauté for 2 to 3 minutes, or until the onion has softened and become translucent. Toss in the carrots and celery and sauté for 2 to 3 minutes. Next, add the garlic, butternut squash, oregano, and rosemary, stir, and sauté for 2 to 3 minutes. Use a splash of veggie broth to deglaze, if the mixture begins to burn against the surface of the pan. Gently tear the maitake mushrooms

recipe continues →

gluten-free

soy-free

apart, add to the pot along with the white pepper, and sauté for 2 to 3 minutes, or until the mushrooms have reduced in size by about half. Pour in all the veggie broth, cover with a lid, lower the heat to a simmer, and cook for 10 to 15 minutes.

② ***Meanwhile, make the dumplings:*** Place the flour in a large bowl, then add the baking powder, salt, and paprika, and stir with a fork until everything is fully incorporated. Add the cold butter and use the fork to smash and press it into mini balls throughout the dough. Slowly stir ¼ cup (60 ml) of the plant-based milk at a time into the flour mixture. Once all the milk is incorporated, dump the dough out onto a large, clean cutting board and press flat to a 1-inch thickness. Cut into 1-inch pieces and transfer to a clean plate. If it's warm in the kitchen, you can place the plate in the fridge for 5 to 10 minutes, to help chill the vegan butter inside the dumplings.

③ When the butternut squash in the soup is fork-tender, add the dumplings to the pot and cook for 5 minutes, or until they expand and double in size. Remove from the heat and set aside. Let cool for 5 minutes before serving. To plate, add a generous amount of soup broth and veggies into each individual bowl, then top with three to five dumplings. Enjoy immediately while warm. This soup is best served immediately, but it will keep for 2 to 3 days in the fridge.

gluten-free soy-free

Save the Sea-Food CHOWDER

serves 4 or 5

When I was living in San Francisco, chowder bread bowls were a weekly occurrence. I would always head to the pier or sit on the patio of a local café and have a date with the city. There's nothing like having a whole, uninterrupted bread bowl of chowder to yourself while you watch the city buzz around. This chowder is an ode to the city that raised me, and a reminder of the ocean that we desperately need to save us. Ditching seafood is right up there on the list of saving the planet with ditching dairy, and this chowder is the first step to realizing you never needed the clams in the chowder to begin with, not when you have mushrooms and hearts of palm. Not all chowder is meant to be eaten alone, so call a few friends and save the sea together.

THE GOODS

4 cups (960 ml) veggie broth, plus 3 tablespoons (45 ml) veggie broth or water
1 onion, diced
1 teaspoon salt
2 medium-size carrots, diced
3 celery ribs, medium diced
4 garlic cloves, sliced
1 pound (225 g) small red potatoes, sliced
1 teaspoon mustard powder
1 teaspoon ground coriander
4 ounces (110 g) oyster mushrooms, torn apart
4 ounces (110 g) king oyster mushrooms, sliced
1 (8-ounce [220 g]) can hearts of palm, rinsed and sliced
½ teaspoon ground white pepper
1 teaspoon kelp flakes
1 bay leaf
2 cups (480 ml) Whole Milk (page 46), or 1 batch Protein Hero Crema (page 129)
1½ teaspoons (7.5 ml) Cholula hot sauce, plus more for garnish
½ teaspoon paprika
2 tablespoons (6 g) chopped fresh chives, plus more for garnish
4 or 5 vegan sourdough or gluten-free bread bowls

THE METHOD

① Preheat the oven to 350°F (177°C). Heat a large soup pot on the stove over medium heat. Once hot, put in the 3 tablespoons (45 ml) of veggie broth, the onion, and salt. Sauté for about 1 minute, add the carrots and celery, and sauté for another minute. Add the garlic and sauté for another minute. Toss in the potatoes, sprinkle in the mustard powder and coriander, and toast the spices, stirring,

recipe continues →

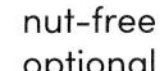
nut-free optional

gluten-free optional

soy-free optional

oil-free

for 2 to 3 minutes. If the mixture starts to stick to the surface of the pan, you can use a splash of veggie broth to deglaze. Next, add the mushrooms, hearts of palm, white pepper, and kelp flakes, and sauté for another 2 to 3 minutes. Pour in the 4 cups (960 ml) of veggie broth, add the bay leaf, cover, and simmer on low for 10 to 15 minutes, or until the potatoes are fork-tender. Then pour in the milk, add the Cholula, paprika, and chives, cook for 1 to 2 minutes, then remove from the heat. Cover and set aside.

② While the soup is cooking, prepare your bread bowls by cutting off the tops and scooping out the center of each loaf, then bake for 5 to 10 minutes. When your bread bowls are toasted to your desired liking, serve with a generous amount of chowder in each bowl. Garnish with chopped chives and more hot sauce. The soup will store, in a container, for 4 to 5 days in the fridge—just be sure to prepare your bread bowls right when you're ready to eat!

nut-free optional

gluten-free optional

soy-free optional

oil-free

Oven-Roasted LASAGNA SOUP

serves 4 or 5

We get so hooked on a certain food because of the love and care it gave us at a certain point of our life. It's not necessarily the fact that it has dairy, or meat, or veggies; it's the reminder of the person who first made it for us, and the memories that we hold on to by keeping the recipe alive. This soup is just that. It's love in a bowl. It has the feeling that our grandma made it, hits every single spot—creamy, a little peppery, comforting—and truly makes everything feel right in the world. Not to mention, this is a lazy gal's lasagna, so what isn't there to love?

THE GOODS

2 red bell peppers, seeded and sliced
1 garlic bulb, top sliced off
1 onion, sliced
½ cup (90 g) cashews or blanched almonds
2 tablespoons (30 ml) olive oil
2 teaspoons salt
¾ teaspoon freshly ground black pepper
1 leek, tops removed and discarded, sliced
3 large portobello mushrooms, stems removed and discarded, sliced
4 to 5 tomatoes, small chopped, or 1 (15-ounce [425 g]) can diced tomatoes
1 (15-ounce [425 g]) can cannellini beans, rinsed
8 cups (1.9 L) veggie broth
1 cup (240 ml) unsweetened plant-based milk
1 (13- to 14-ounce [370–400 g]) package of your favorite lasagna noodles (GF if needed)
2 cups (50 g) chopped kale
1 cup (15 g) chopped fresh basil

THE METHOD

① Preheat the oven to 350°F (177°C). Combine the bell peppers, garlic bulb, onion, and cashews on a large baking sheet. Drizzle with 1 tablespoon (15 ml) of the olive oil, sprinkle with half of the salt and half of the black pepper, then mix well with your hands. Spread the mixture into a single layer and bake for 25 to 30 minutes, or until the garlic is golden brown and bell peppers are soft. Once done, remove from the oven and set aside.

recipe continues →

cashew-free optional

gluten-free optional

soy-free

② While the veggies bake, place a 7-quart soup pot over medium heat. Once hot, add the remaining tablespoon (15 ml) of olive oil, leek, and remaining salt and black pepper, and sauté for 1 minute. Next, add the portobello mushrooms and cook for 3 to 4 minutes, or until the portobellos are softened. Add the tomatoes, and stir to deglaze the pan. Add the cannellini beans, stir, then add veggie broth and bring to a boil.

③ Meanwhile, transfer the roasted onion, cashews, and bell peppers to a high-powered blender. Squeeze the garlic cloves into the blender from the bulb and add the plant-based milk. Blend on high speed for 30 seconds, or until smooth. Set aside.

④ Once the veggie broth is boiling, lower the heat slightly, pour the creamy blended mixture into the pot, and stir. Break your uncooked lasagna noodles into half or thirds (depending on your preference), add them to the boiling soup, and cook for the duration of their package instructions. Once the noodles are soft and tender, add the kale and basil, and mix well. Taste for salt. The soup will be done when the kale has softened. Enjoy immediately.

cashew-free optional

gluten-free optional

soy-free

Rainbow Rajas con Crema

serves 2 or 3

Onions, charred peppers, cream, and corn make a magical combo worthy of breakfast, lunch, and dinner. This Mexican dish was originally introduced to me when I was working in Mexico in my early twenties. It was love at first taste and I had to have it all the time. The only problem was, once I gave up dairy, I could never find it dairy-free while traveling. So here it is, my ode to *rajas con crema* with a little twist. I added bell peppers, sliced purple cabbage, and a tofu crema to make this a complete meal. All you need now are some freshly made tortillas and a cinnamon coffee.

THE GOODS

3 bell peppers (one each green, yellow, and red)
2 poblano peppers
2 tablespoons (30 ml) veggie broth
1 onion, sliced
1½ teaspoons salt
3 garlic cloves, peeled and sliced
½ cup (35 g) thinly sliced purple cabbage
1 cup (140 g) fresh or frozen corn kernels
1 teaspoon dried coriander
¼ teaspoon freshly grated nutmeg
½ (14-ounce [400 g]) block firm tofu
½ cup (120 ml) unsweetened plant-based milk
1 tablespoon (5 g) nutritional yeast
2 tablespoons (30 ml) freshly squeezed lemon juice
1 tablespoon (15 ml) white wine vinegar

THE METHOD

① First, blister all your peppers, whole, over a lit gas burner, or grill them, to roast and blacken the skins. Use tongs to turn the peppers, to get each side nice and toasted. If you don't have a gas stove or grill, you can put them on a baking sheet and place in a broiler set to HIGH, turning every 3 minutes until they're blackened on each side. Once they're all toasted and black, immediately place them in a heatproof bowl, cover with

recipe continues →

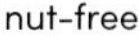
nut-free

gluten-free

grain-free

oil-free

a lid, and let steam for about 10 minutes. This is a great time to get the rest of your ingredients prepped and ready to go.

② Once they've steamed, use your fingers to scrape or wipe off and discard the blackened parts of the skin of each pepper. I like to do this near the sink so I can wash my hands. Cut all the peppers in half, remove the seeds and stems, and then thinly slice. Set aside.

③ In a large, deep sauté pan over medium heat, combine the veggie broth, onion, and 1 teaspoon of the salt. Sauté until the onion is soft, for about 3 minutes. You can add a dash more veggie broth if the onion begins to burn against the surface of the pan. Next, add the sliced peppers and sauté for 1 to 2 minutes. Add the garlic, cabbage, corn, coriander, and nutmeg, and cook on medium-low, stirring frequently, for about 5 minutes. When done, remove from the heat but keep the veggies in the pan.

④ Next, make your creamy sauce: Combine the tofu, plant-based milk, nutritional yeast, lemon juice, white wine vinegar, and the remaining ½ teaspoon of the salt in a high-powered blender. Blend on high speed until smooth, for about 20 seconds.

⑤ Pour the creamy sauce into the pan of veggies and stir well. Cook over medium-low heat, stirring, for 4 to 5 minutes, or until the sauce reduces slightly. Be sure to check at this point for your salt and spice preferences. Remove from the heat, and leave the pan covered to keep it warm. Serve with warm tortillas, inside tamales, or as a side dish to your favorite Mexican-inspired feast. Stores for 3 to 4 days in the fridge.

nut-free

gluten-free

grain-free

oil-free

CHILES RELLENOS

serves 5 or 6

If a date is making you chiles rellenos from scratch, you better believe you have exited the casual stage or the friend zone and coasted right on into commitment. Chiles rellenos is a love language all its own, and since finding a dairy-free relleno is next to impossible, it's time you took this dish home. I paired it with my Mozzarella (page 108), so be sure to prep the cheese the night before, to have it ready to go for date night. Make these for two and you'll have the most epic leftovers for chile relleno burritos the next day. It's the date night that just keeps on giving.

THE GOODS

- 5 to 6 poblano peppers
- 1 block Mozzarella (page 108), sliced
- 1½ cups (225 g) 1-to-1 gluten-free flour or all-purpose flour
- 1 teaspoon salt
- 1 teaspoon chili powder
- ½ cup (120 ml) unsweetened plant-based milk
- ¾ cup (180 ml) sparkling water
- ¼ cup (60 ml) avocado oil
- Guajillo Sauce (page 130)

THE METHOD

① Turn on a gas burner, place the peppers on the open flame, and blister them on all sides. If you don't have a gas stove, you can pop them into the oven with the broiler set to HIGH. Turn the peppers every 2 minutes to blacken the sides. When all the sides are blistered, place them in a big heatproof bowl, cover with a lid, and let them sweat for 5 to 7 minutes. Gently wipe away most of the black blistered skin from the peppers without breaking through to the inside. It doesn't have to be perfect; just get as much of the blackened skin off as you can.

② Make a single slit down the side of each pepper. Carefully remove the seeds, and stuff about ½ cup (120 ml) of the mozzarella into each pepper. Carefully close each pepper with three or four wooden toothpicks to hold them closed.

recipe continues →

gluten-free optional

soy-free

3 Combine the flour, salt, and chili powder in a large bowl, and stir until fully mixed. Pour in the plant-based milk and sparkling water, and stir with a fork until you have a thick batter.

4 Next, heat the avocado oil in a large cast-iron skillet over medium-high heat. Then gently dip the stuffed poblanos into the batter, and lay them in the hot oil. Cook on each side for 60 to 90 seconds, or until golden brown. I like to use a fish spatula to flip and repeat for all three to four sides of the peppers. When all the sides are crispy, including the top, remove from the pan, remove the toothpicks, and serve immediately with guajillo sauce.

gluten-free optional

soy-free

Burrata PESTO SANDO

makes 4 sandwiches

This sandwich is all you need, and more: fluffy yet toasty ciabatta, decadent pistachio pesto, marinated and caramelized peppers and mushrooms, and a silky homemade burrata cheese that'll make you wonder why you didn't go through with the breakup sooner. Pairs perfectly with a picnic at the park and a bottle of bubbly.

THE GOODS

Veggies:

- 2 tablespoons (30 ml) olive oil (optional)
- 3 large portobello mushrooms, sliced
- 1 red bell pepper, seeded and sliced
- ½ teaspoon salt
- 2 tablespoons (30 ml) balsamic vinegar
- 1 tablespoon (15 ml) Dijon mustard
- 1 tablespoon (15 ml) freshly squeezed lemon juice
- 1 tablespoon (15 ml) pure maple syrup
- ½ teaspoon freshly ground black pepper
- 2 handfuls arugula

Pistachio Pesto:

- 2 cups (70 g) packed fresh basil
- ½ cup (30 g) packed fresh dill
- 2 garlic cloves
- ¼ cup (40 g) shelled pistachios or hulled sunflower seeds
- ¼ cup (60 ml) water
- 1 teaspoon lemon zest
- 1 tablespoon (15 ml) freshly squeezed lemon juice
- 3 tablespoons (45 ml) high-quality olive oil
- ½ teaspoon salt
- ½ teaspoon freshly ground black pepper

For Serving:

- Burrata cheese balls (page 108)
- 1 large vegan ciabatta loaf (GF if needed)

THE METHOD

① *Cook the veggies:* Heat 2 tablespoons (30 ml) of water (or the olive oil, if using), in a large sauté pan over medium-high heat. Add the mushrooms, bell pepper, and salt, and cook the veggies for 1 to 2 minutes, to soften slightly. Add the balsamic vinegar, Dijon, lemon juice, maple syrup, and black pepper, and cook for 3 to 4 more minutes. Once the veggies are soft, remove from the heat.

② *Make the pesto:* Combine everything for the pesto in a high-powered blender and blend on high speed for 30 to 45 seconds, or until it's almost

recipe continues →

gluten-free optional

soy-free

oil-free optional

smooth but not fully pureed. Pour into a bowl and set aside. If you love this pesto as much as I do, double the recipe and store in an airtight mason jar for up to a week!

③ To build the sandwich, cut the ciabatta loaf in half horizontally and toast the bread either on a cast-iron skillet or in the oven on BROIL for a minute or two. Add a generous amount of pesto to each slice; then on the lower portion of the bread, layer the veggies, the arugula, and then the burrata. Top the sandwich with the top portion of the bread and cut into four pieces. Enjoy immediately while warm.

gluten-free optional

soy-free

oil-free optional

One-Pot Meyer Lemon CACIO E PEPE

serves 2 or 3

If you're in college, or live in a tiny space, or just hate doing dishes, or—let's face it—love pasta, this one is for you. *Cacio e pepe* is everywhere, and for good reason—it hits all the spots. Pasta, cheese, and pepper are always a good idea and have a vibe that doesn't need much explanation. All you need for this one is one pot and a blender for the Pourable Mozzarella (page 88). It tastes as good as at that bougie Italian restaurant in your neighborhood, but can be made at home for a quarter of the price—and the mess.

THE GOODS

4 cups (960 ml) veggie broth
1 cup (240 ml) unsweetened No-Strain Almond Milk (page 42) or store-bought unsweetened plant-milk of choice
1 teaspoon salt
12 to 13 ounces (375 g) dried spaghetti or tagliatelle, or brown rice penne pasta for GF option
½ cup (120 ml) Pourable Mozzarella (page 88)
2 tablespoons (30 ml) freshly squeezed lemon juice
1 teaspoon freshly ground black pepper
Potato Parmesan (page 95), shaved, for the top
Fresh basil leaves

THE METHOD

Combine the veggie broth, almond milk, and salt in a deep saucepan. Cover and cook over medium heat until boiling, for 4 to 5 minutes. Don't walk away while it cooks because it will boil over quick! Then add the pasta and cook for about 7 minutes, or until al dente. How long it cooks will depend on what pasta brand you use, so keep an eye on it after 5 minutes! Once the pasta is reaching al dente, add the pourable mozzarella and cook for another minute. If you still have residual liquid, the mozzarella will help it thicken. Remove from the heat and let sit for 2 to 3 minutes with the lid on. Then, add the lemon juice and pepper, and mix thoroughly. Once ready to serve, place a generous amount on each plate, and garnish with shaved Parm and basil leaves.

nut-free optional

gluten-free optional

soy-free

oil-free

LODGE

Lemon Poppy Seed SCALLOPED POTATOES

makes one 9 x 9-inch pan

To be real, I could forgo making this for anyone else and seat myself on the couch to eat this entire pan of scalloped potatoes. Since finding love in a pan of potatoes might not be enough for you, sharing this will be okay too. These scalloped potatoes are not only healthier than the classic, but the flavor is even better too. You can use either base for the Crema (page 129): if you want it to be high in protein and low in fat, go with the Protein Hero; if you want this to be a luscious dish for the holidays or a dinner party, use the Indulgent Queen as the base. Either way, your view on scalloped potatoes will never be the same.

THE GOODS

6 large russet potatoes, washed and peeled
½ cup (120 ml) plant-based milk of choice
1 batch Dill Poppy Seed Crema (page 129)
2 cups (40 g) chopped kale
½ teaspoon flaky sea salt
¼ teaspoon freshly ground black pepper
1 teaspoon nutritional yeast

THE METHOD

1. Preheat your oven to 350°F (177°C).

2. Use a mandoline to slice all the potatoes. Set aside. Combine your plant-based milk and crema in a large bowl, and stir until fully mixed. Grab a 9 x 9-inch baking pan and spread ½ cup (60 ml) of the crema mixture in the pan. Add a layer of potato slices until it covers the surface, layer a handful of kale over that. Continue in this order until you have three or four layers, ending with a layer of crema on top, and have used all the ingredients.

3. Sprinkle with the flaky sea salt, pepper, and nutritional yeast. Bake, covered, for 45 minutes, then 30 more minutes, uncovered. Remove from the oven and let cool for 5 minutes before serving. Leftovers will keep for 3 to 4 days in the fridge.

nut-free optional

gluten-free

soy-free optional

grain-free

oil-free

LINGUINE and CLAMS

serves 3 or 4

This is the pasta that can turn a Tuesday date night into a proposal—it's that good! Linguine and clams are so easy to make plant-based by swapping out the clams for trumpet mushrooms and using ground nori to really go all in on the seafood vibe. This recipe is perfect for beginner cooks and is the best weeknight meal. Don't forget to prep the Potato Parm (page 95) ahead of time because this really isn't the same without it. Regardless of whether you're ending the night with a bellyful of pasta or a proposal, you know a night with linguine and clams is always a night to remember.

THE GOODS

1 (1-pound [454g]) package dried linguine pasta (GF if needed)
Your choice: a splash of veggie broth, pasta water, or olive oil, for cooked pasta
3 tablespoons (45 g) vegan salted butter (see the Butter Block, page 122)
1 shallot, peeled and sliced
4 garlic cloves, peeled and sliced
1 teaspoon salt
6 ounces (165 g) trumpet mushrooms, rough chopped
½ teaspoon freshly ground black pepper
1 cup (240 ml) white wine
1 teaspoon ground nori
1 cup (240 ml) unsweetened plant-based milk of choice

For Garnish:
Chopped fresh parsley
Potato Parmesan (page 95)
Red pepper flakes

THE METHOD

① Fill a large soup pot with water and cook the noodles according to the package instructions. When you drain the pasta, reserve 1 cup (240 ml) of the pasta water for later. Place the cooked noodles back into the empty pot with a splash of veggie broth, pasta water, or olive oil to prevent any sticking. Set aside.

② Heat a large sauté pan over medium heat. Then put in the vegan butter and shallot and sauté for 1 minute. Add the garlic and ½ teaspoon of the

recipe continues →

gluten-free optional

soy-free

salt, and sauté for 1 minute more. Add the trumpet mushrooms and pepper, and sauté over medium-high heat for 3 to 4 minutes, or until the mushrooms turn a bit golden brown. Pour in the wine to deglaze the pan and let cook for about 3 minutes, or until the liquid has reduced by half. Add the nori, and sauté for another minute. Add the plant-based milk, reserved pasta water, and remaining ½ teaspoon of salt, cover, and simmer for 3 to 4 minutes. Remove from the heat and set aside until ready to serve.

③ To plate, place a generous amount of noodles in the center of each individual serving bowl, and then ladle three to five splashes of the "clam" and butter mixture over the noodles. Garnish with fresh parsley, a whole bunch of Potato Parm, and red pepper flakes. Leftovers will keep for 2 to 3 days in the fridge.

gluten-free optional

soy-free

Creamy Black Garlic RAMEN

serves 4

This recipe's flavor profile is so complex and so freakin' creamy, I promise you will blow your own mind when you make this. It's the best pairing for a rainy night in and will leave you desperate to get every last drop. If you can, meal prep the broth the day before so it can build flavor overnight while it sits in the fridge. Like a fine wine, this broth really does get better with time. Make it with black sesame seed milk or coconut—dealer's choice.

THE GOODS

Tofu:
1 (14-ounce [400 g]) block tofu, pressed and cut into 1-inch cubes
1 tablespoon (15 g) sesame seed oil
½ teaspoon salt
½ teaspoon granulated garlic

Broth:
1 tablespoon (15 ml) sesame seed oil
1 large onion, thinly sliced
1 teaspoon salt
1 tablespoon (5 g) peeled and minced fresh ginger
1 tablespoon (15 g) black garlic puree or minced regular garlic
2 tablespoons (30 ml) liquid aminos
3 heaping tablespoons (60 g) miso paste
3 heaping tablespoons (45 g) tomato paste
1 teaspoon sriracha or hot sauce
4 cups (960 ml) Black Sesame Seed Milk (page 57) or full-fat Coconut Milk (page 49; canned works too)
4 cups (960 ml) veggie broth

Veggies:
1 tablespoon (15 ml) sesame seed oil
¼ cup (60 ml) coconut aminos
1 teaspoon sriracha
4 portobello mushrooms, sliced in half
2 baby bok choy, cut into quarters or in half

nut-free

gluten-free optional

Ramen:
1 (24-ounce [680 g]) package ramen noodles (GF if needed)

For Garnish (optional):
Sesame seeds
Chili oil

THE METHOD

① *Make the tofu:* Preheat your oven to 400°F (205°C). Place the tofu in a bowl and toss with the sesame seed oil, salt, and granulated garlic until evenly coated. Space the tofu equally apart on a parchment paper– or

recipe continues →

silicone mat–lined baking sheet, and bake for 25 to 30 minutes, or until golden brown. Pro tip: don't forget to shake the tofu halfway through baking, to prevent it from sticking later on.

② ***While the tofu bakes, make the broth:*** Place a soup pot over medium heat. Once the pot is hot, put in the sesame seed oil, onion, and salt, and sauté for 3 to 4 minutes until the onion becomes translucent and fragrant. Add the ginger, black garlic puree, liquid aminos, miso paste, tomato paste, and sriracha, and cook for 1 to 2 more minutes while stirring to coat the onion. Add your black sesame milk and cook for 2 to 3 minutes more. Pour in the veggie broth and lower the heat to a simmer. Cook, covered, over medium-low heat for 10 minutes.

③ ***Meanwhile marinate the veggies:*** Combine the sesame seed oil, coconut aminos, and sriracha in a large bowl. Immerse the mushrooms and bok choy in the mixture.

④ ***Back to the broth:*** Give the broth a good stir and then continue to cook for 15 more minutes, covered, over medium-low heat.

⑤ While the broth simmers, heat a large cast-iron skillet or flattop over medium-high heat. Then remove your mushroom halves from their marinade and sauté until soft and cooked down. Use tongs to flip the mushrooms; and this step can get a bit smoky, so have a fan on. Remove the mushrooms from the pan and set aside. Repeat with the bok choy until all its sides are seared golden brown.

⑥ Fill a separate empty large soup pot with salted water and bring to a boil. Then cook your ramen noodles according to the package instructions. Drain. Add the cooked ramen noodles back to the hot empty pot and stir with a dash of veggie broth or sesame seed oil. Set aside.

⑦ To serve, place a generous amount of noodles in a large individual soup bowl, and then add a few ladlefuls of broth, garnish with a slice or two of mushrooms, a quarter of bok choy, and a few cubes of cooked tofu. Optionally, garnish with sesame seeds and chili oil.

nut-free

gluten-free optional

MUSHROOM STROGANOFF & Fluffy Potatoes

serves 4 or 5

This recipe has been in my roster for years. It was my secret weapon to get my husband to finally get his life together and actually commit when we were just a fling so many years ago. To put so much weight on a stroganoff and some potatoes seems insane, but I promise you, this recipe is truly that good. Pick your Crema base and then use half for the potatoes and half for the finishing touch of the stroganoff. You won't miss the dairy, you won't miss the beef, and you'll become as obsessed as my husband.

THE GOODS

Fluffy Potatoes:

10 yellow potatoes, quartered
1 tablespoon salt
3 garlic cloves, peeled and sliced
½ batch plain crema (page 129)
½ teaspoon freshly ground black pepper
¼ cup (60 ml) Oat Hemp Milk (page 45) or store-bought unsweetened plant milk of choice
1 teaspoon granulated garlic
¼ cup (10 g) minced fresh parsley
1 tablespoon (3 g) minced fresh chives, plus more for garnish

Stroganoff:

1½ teaspoons (7.5 ml) olive oil
1 medium-size onion, diced
1½ teaspoons salt
4 garlic cloves, peeled and minced
12 ounces (335 g) large portobello mushrooms, sliced
4 ounces (110 g) shiitake mushrooms
1 tablespoon (2 g) fresh or dried thyme
½ teaspoon freshly ground black pepper
2 cup (480 ml) unsweetened Oat Hemp Milk (page 45)
½ cup (120 ml) veggie broth
For slurry: 1 tablespoon (7 g) tapioca starch + 2 tablespoons (30 ml) water
½ batch plain crema (page 129)
Fresh parsley, as garnish

recipe continues →

nut-free optional

gluten-free

soy-free optional

grain-free optional

THE METHOD

① *Make the fluffy potatoes:* Place the potatoes in a large soup pot before you fill it three-quarters full with water. Add 1½ teaspoons of the salt and the garlic to the water, and bring to a boil. Boil until the potatoes are fork-tender, for about 15 minutes. Once the potatoes are soft, remove from the heat and carefully drain away the water, being careful to keep the potatoes and garlic in the pot. With a potato masher, smash them into a smooth consistency. Add the half batch of crema, 1 teaspoon of the remaining salt, pepper, Oat Hemp Milk, granulated garlic, parsley, and chives, and stir them into the smashed potatoes. Taste for seasoning. Cover with a lid to keep warm. Set aside.

② *Now for the stroganoff:* Heat the olive oil in a large saucepan over medium-high heat. Once the oil is hot, add the onion and 1 teaspoon of the salt, and sauté for 2 to 3 minutes. When the onion becomes soft and slightly translucent, add the garlic and sauté for another 1 to 2 minutes. Use a splash of veggie broth, if needed, to deglaze the pan. Toss in the mushrooms, dried thyme, remaining ½ teaspoon of salt, and the pepper, and slowly cook down for 3 to 4 minutes. It will seem like a lot, but they will reduce in size by almost half. When all the mushrooms are soft and reduced, add the Oat Hemp Milk and veggie broth and cook down, stirring, for 2 to 3 minutes. Cover with a lid, lower the heat to a simmer, and cook for 5 to 7 minutes.

③ While the stroganoff simmers, create the slurry by stirring together the tapioca starch and water in a small bowl. Remove the lid, and stir in the other half batch of crema and the slurry mixture, and cook for 1 to 2 minutes on medium-high heat. Taste for salt and check the consistency; it should be silky and creamy. Remove from the heat and cover with a lid to keep warm.

④ To serve, place a generous amount of fluffy potatoes in an individual serving bowl, and then ladle one to three scoops of stroganoff over the top. Garnish with fresh parsley and serve immediately. Store the potatoes and the gravy in separate containers in the fridge for 5 days.

nut-free optional

gluten-free

soy-free optional

grain-free optional

BIRRIA TACOS

makes 8 tacos

In San Diego, *birria* tacos are *everywhere* and pretty much available 24/7 because, let's be real, who doesn't love tacos smothered with cheese at 3:00 a.m.? Unfortunately, they're almost impossible to find without meat, let alone without cheese. You'll be in shock when you eat these because not only are they so meaty, but the Cheddar cheese will make you question everything. Unlike any other taco, you make these by dipping your tortilla in the savory chili broth and then searing it with the cheese and mushrooms inside. It's a literal flavor explosion with cheesy meltiness to match. Finally, no matter where you are, you, too, can get birria tacos for those late-night munchies.

THE GOODS

Birria Sauce:

2 to 3 dried guajillo peppers, stems removed
3½ cups (840 ml) veggie broth
1 teaspoon olive oil, plus 1 tablespoon (15 ml) for finishing
1 onion, peeled and sliced
1½ teaspoons salt
2 garlic cloves, peeled and sliced
1 teaspoon ground cumin
2 teaspoons dried oregano
1 teaspoon chili powder
½ teaspoon ground cinnamon
½ teaspoon freshly ground black pepper

Mushrooms:

16 ounces (450 g) oyster mushrooms, torn into smaller pieces
½ teaspoon salt
1 teaspoon granulated garlic
1 teaspoon paprika
2 teaspoons olive oil
2 teaspoons agave nectar

Tacos:

8 corn tortillas
Cheddar block (page 87)

THE METHOD

① *Make the birria sauce:* Soak the guajillo peppers in 1 cup (240 ml) of the veggie broth for 10 to 20 minutes. Set aside. Combine the teaspoon of olive oil, onion, and 1 teaspoon of the salt in a medium-size saucepan over medium heat. Sauté for about 3 minutes, or until the onion starts to soften and brown. Add the garlic and sauté for about 1 minute. Next, add the cumin, oregano, chili powder, cinnamon, and black pepper, and sauté for 1 to 2 minutes. Remove from the heat and set aside.

recipe continues →

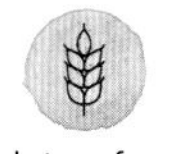

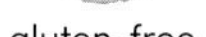
gluten-free

soy-free

② Next, transfer the two rehydrated guajillos and the broth they were soaking in to a high-powered blender, along with the cooked onion, plus an additional cup (240 ml) of veggie broth. Blend on high speed for 60 seconds, or until fully smooth. Pour the mixture back into the saucepan and simmer, covered, over low heat for 15 minutes.

③ Now, remove the lid, stir in 1 cup (240 ml) of the remaining veggie broth and the remaining ½ teaspoon of salt, and then simmer, covered, over low heat for another 15 minutes, checking every few minutes to make sure it's not burning. Then, remove from the heat, drizzle the tablespoon (15 ml) of olive oil over the top, and stir in the remaining ½ cup (120 ml) of veggie broth. Taste for salt and spiciness. Remove from the heat and set aside.

④ *Make the mushrooms:* Heat a large cast-iron skillet over medium-high heat. Then, put in the mushrooms and salt, and sauté for 3 to 4 minutes, or until they reduce in size. Add the granulated garlic, paprika, olive oil, and agave, and cook down for 1 to 2 minutes. Remove from the heat, toss the cooked mushrooms into a bowl, and set aside.

⑤ *Prepare the tacos:* While the cast-iron skillet is still hot, lower the heat to medium-low, grab a tortilla, and dip it into the birria sauce until it's fully submerged. Quickly and carefully place the soaked tortilla on the hot skillet, and add a spoonful of cooked mushrooms to one-half of the tortilla and ¼ cup (30 g) of shredded Cheddar to the other half. After about 10 seconds, fold the cheese side over onto the mushrooms. Cook each side for 1 to 2 minutes, or until fully seared golden brown on each side. Serve immediately while still hot. Serve with a ramekin filled with the broth. Enjoy! If you have leftovers, store the finished tacos in an airtight container for up to 5 days, and reheat by searing on the cast-iron skillet with a dash of oil for 30 seconds on each side.

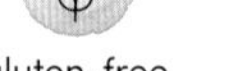
gluten-free

soy-free

PANEER MASALA

serves 4 or 5

Indian curry with paneer is something I have been craving for years and something I haven't been able to get dairy-free literally anywhere. And I'm not talking about replacing the cheese with tofu; I'm talking about a real paneer masala that has a cheese worth licking the bowl over. Making a dairy-free paneer that will hold up in a curry was no easy task, but the paneer (page 114) is the absolute perfect cheese for this curry. This dish is complex, so delicious, and is my way of bringing this already vegetarian dish fully over to the plant-based world.

THE GOODS

1 tablespoon (15 g) vegan butter (see the Butter Block, page 122)
1½ teaspoons garam masala
1 teaspoon chili powder
½ teaspoon fennel seeds
1 medium-size yellow onion, chopped
1 teaspoon salt
1 bay leaf
3 garlic cloves, minced
1 teaspoon minced fresh ginger
1 tablespoon (15 g) tomato paste
¼ cup (35 g) cashews
4 tomatoes, chopped, or 1 (15-ounce [425 g]) can diced tomatoes
1 tablespoon (10 g) coconut sugar
1¾ cups (420 ml) Coconut Milk (page 49), or canned full-fat coconut milk
Paneer (page 114), cut into 1-inch cubes
Cooked basmati rice, for serving

THE METHOD

① Heat a large, heavy-bottomed saucepan over medium-low heat. Put in the butter, garam masala, chili powder, and fennel seeds, and toast the spices for 3 to 4 minutes. Next, add the onion, salt and bay leaf, and sauté for 2 to 3 minutes. When the onion has softened, toss in the garlic and ginger, and sauté for 2 to 3 minutes over medium-low heat. Stir in the tomato paste and cashews, then sauté for 60 seconds. Toss in the tomatoes to help deglaze the pan. Sprinkle the coconut sugar over the top, then add half the coconut milk. Cover and cook over medium heat for 10 to 15 minutes, stirring occasionally. Remove from the heat and stir in the remaining coconut milk.

② Transfer to a high-powered blender and blend until smooth, or you can blend in the pan with an immersion blender—up to you! Once you have a super-creamy curry, pour it back into the saucepan and add the paneer.

③ Mix well and serve immediately, while still warm, with basmati rice. If there are leftovers, store the rice separately from the masala and keep it in an airtight container in the fridge for 5 to 6 days.

gluten-free

Home-Style SQUASH POTPIE

makes one 9-inch pie

If you haven't had the chance yet to make the incredible Home-Style Gravy (page 142), you're in luck, because this potpie gives you something besides biscuits or a piece of chicken-fried tofu to enjoy the gravy with. I use spelt for the crust here to make this potpie nutrient-packed, and if you don't feel like latticing the crust, you can just lay it over the top! Grab a couple of forks, as this potpie is meant to be enjoyed right out of the pan.

THE GOODS

Crust:

- 3 cups (420 g) spelt, all-purpose, or whole wheat flour
- 2 teaspoons salt
- 1 teaspoon coconut sugar
- 1 cup (120 g) cubed cold butter (see the Butter Block, page 122)
- 1 tablespoon (15 ml) apple cider vinegar
- 12 to 14 tablespoons (180 to 210 ml) cold water
- ¼ cup (60 ml) unsweetened plant-based milk
- 1 tablespoon (8 g) sesame seeds

Potpie Filling:

- 3 tablespoons (45 ml) olive oil
- 1 onion, peeled and small diced
- 1 teaspoon salt
- ½ cup (55 g) minced celery
- 2 cups (260 g) peeled, seeded, and medium-diced butternut squash
- ½ cup (60 g) small-diced carrot
- 4 garlic cloves, minced
- 3 cups (720 ml) No-Strain Almond Milk (page 42); for nut-free, use Oat Hemp Milk (page 45)
- 1 tablespoon (2 g) fresh thyme leaves
- ¾ cup (75 g) ground walnuts
- 1 cup (70 g) shaved broccoli
- 2 tablespoons (6 g) chopped fresh parsley

recipe continues →

soy-free

THE METHOD

① *Make the crust:* Combine the spelt flour, salt, coconut sugar, and butter in a food processor and blend on high speed for 30 seconds, or until small balls of dough begin to form. Add the apple cider vinegar and water, 1 tablespoon (15 ml) at a time, while processing on low speed. You may need less or more water depending on your climate and altitude. Once the dough is tacky and holds together when you press it between your fingers, remove the dough from the food processor and form it into a ball. Wrap the ball of dough in parchment paper and place in the fridge to chill for 45 minutes.

② *While the dough chills, make the filling:* Heat the olive oil in a large sauté pan over medium-high heat. Once the oil is hot, add the onion and salt, and sauté for 2 to 3 minutes. Then, add the celery, butternut squash, and carrot, and sauté for 3 to 4 minutes, or until the veggies start to soften. Toss in the garlic and sauté for another 1 to 2 minutes. Next, pour in the almond milk and stir. Lower the heat to medium-low and cook, uncovered, for 10 minutes while the liquid reduces by about half. Now, add the thyme, walnuts, and broccoli, and cook for 2 to 3 more minutes. Remove from the heat, stir in the parsley, and let the filling cool with the lid removed. Don't worry if it's a bit liquidy or thin; as it sits, it will thicken.

③ Preheat the oven to 400°F (205°C). As the filling cools, it's time to roll out the dough. Grab the ball of dough from the fridge and cut it in half. Place one portion in the center of a large piece of parchment paper, atop a cutting board. Place another large piece of parchment paper on top of the dough, and roll out the dough with a rolling pin. Take your time and roll it out into a flat disk about 1 inch in diameter larger than the size of your pie pan. Remove the top layer of parchment paper, and place your pie pan upside down on top of the rolled-out dough. Now for the tricky part: with one hand holding underneath the cutting board and one under the pie pan, quickly flip everything over, remove the cutting board—

soy-free

and voilà! the dough should be in the pan, right side up. Carefully remove the parchment paper, gently press the dough into the pie pan, and fix any imperfections. Set this aside. Now, repeat the rolling-out process with the other dough ball you set aside earlier, rolling it into a size that matches the upper diameter of your pan; this will be the top crust. Set this aside.

④ Pour the filling into the crust-lined pie pan. Take your second rolled-out pie dough, remove the top piece of parchment paper, and carefully flip the dough on top of the filling of the pie. Alternatively, you can lattice the piecrust over the top, by cutting it into strips on its parchment and weaving them across the pie. Whatever you want! Carefully fix the broken edges or imperfections and make it look as beautiful as you are. With a pastry brush, lightly brush the top crust with a layer of plant-based milk and then sprinkle the sesame seeds over the top. Bake for 30 to 35 minutes. Remove from the oven and let cool for 5 to 10 minutes. Serve warm and enjoy! This pie will last in the fridge covered for about 4 days.

soy-free

7. LIFE of the PARTY

HERE'S THE THING. Deep down, I'm a party girl. Behind the matcha, and the yoga, and the breathwork, and the activism, you better believe I love to entertain, to be entertained, and to shake what my momma gave me on the dance floor. I actually think that most chefs are this way behind it all. And, in my opinion, one of the pivotal points in any breakup is getting back out there and showing 'em what you're made of. It's the ultimate test; it's when you could meet someone new, or run into your ex. Or even when you finally feel confident about your dairy-free lifestyle, you turn the corner, and there it is, a cheese board (my personal weakness) or a steaming hot bowl of *queso fundido*. The thing is, you have to come prepared to face whatever is around the corner, and this chapter is about just that. It's about more than having the perfect outfit, it's about having the confidence and showing up fully locked and loaded with what you need to succeed. It's all my favorite party go-tos, like lobster rolls and compound butters for garlic bread, and the perfect pairings with wine, like creamy feta with tomato confit. It's actually not just about coming prepared; it's about creating your own damn party if you want to and showing everyone that not only are you better off for your breakup but they soon will reap the benefits too.

New York–Style Spelt POPPY SEED BAGELS

makes 8 bagels

rising time: 2 hours

There is nothing that can do it quite like a fresh bagel can. These bagels are rustic, healthy, and absolutely delicious. I use spelt flour instead of the typical white bread flour, since it has a higher protein content and is also filled with nutrients like iron and magnesium. It's a bagel that will actually fuel you and your friends too! Pair these with the Roasted Garlic + Scallion Cream Cheese (page 84), tomatoes, capers, and pickled onions, for the most epic brunch board worthy of a crowd.

THE GOODS

1 (0.25-ounce [7 g]) packet active dry yeast
1½ tablespoons (12 g) coconut sugar (sub organic cane sugar for coconut allergy)
1½ cups (360 ml) warm water (about 105°F [41°C])
1½ teaspoons pink salt
3¼ cups (460 g) spelt flour, plus 1 tablespoon (9 g) for kneading and more for dusting
1 tablespoon (15 ml) olive oil
1½ teaspoons baking soda
1 tablespoon agave nectar
3 to 4 tablespoons (30 g) poppy seeds
Roasted Garlic + Scallion Cream Cheese (page 84) or Strawberry Cheesecake Cream Cheese (page 84)

THE METHOD

① Combine the active dry yeast, coconut sugar, and warm water—make sure the water is hot to the touch, but not too hot so that you can't keep your finger submerged—in a stand mixer fitted with the dough hook attachment, or a large bowl. Let sit for about 10 minutes until the yeast "activates"—you'll see a little layer of foam on the top. Once the yeast has foamed, add the pink salt and mix with a fork. Now, add the spelt flour, 1 cup (140 g) at a time, and mix until a dough starts to form. If using a stand mixer, knead on medium speed; if using a bowl, mix with a fork and then transfer to a spelt-floured surface to knead.

② Once a dough starts to form, knead for about 10 more minutes, or until you get a firm but moist dough. You may need to use that extra tablespoon (9 g) of spelt flour or even an extra tablespoon (15 ml) of water to get that perfect dough. Once your dough is smooth, moist, and still tacky without sticking to your fingers, it's ready. Oil a medium-size mixing bowl with the olive oil and add the dough. Cover with a clean, damp towel and let rise for 2 hours.

recipe continues →

nut-free optional

soy-free optional

③ After 2 hours, preheat the oven to 425°F (218°C), line a large baking sheet with parchment paper, and bring a large pot of water to a boil. Then, add the baking soda and agave nectar to the water. Meanwhile, get your bagels ready! The dough should have doubled in size. Lightly punch the dough in the middle, and transfer it from the bowl to a clean surface. The oil from the bowl will help keep it from sticking. Using a bench scraper or a metal spatula, divide the dough ball in half, in half again, and then in half one more time, yielding eight equal-size portions. One by one, using light pressure, roll each portion of dough into a 6-inch rod and then twist it around your fingers to create your bagel! Place on the parchment paper and repeat until no more dough is left.

④ Working in batches of two to four at a time, depending on your pot size, carefully add your bagels to the boiling water. Cook them for 1 minute 45 seconds, then flip them over and cook for another 1 minute 45 seconds on the other side. Remove from the water and place back on the parchment paper with the pretty side up. As you do so, add your poppy seeds while the bagels are still wet. Once all the bagels have been boiled and topped with poppy seeds, bake them for 23 to 25 minutes on their lined baking sheet until golden brown.

⑤ Remove from the oven and let cool for at least 15 minutes before digging in. Keep them on a dark spot on the counter in a sealed container for 3 to 5 days if they last that long! Serve with your favorite cream cheese (see page 84). Freeze in an air-sealed freezer-safe bag for 2 to 3 weeks.

nut-free optional

soy-free optional

Breakfast PIZZA POCKETS with Hollandaise

makes 8 pizza pockets

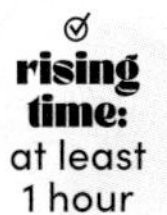

When the ultimate meal prep could also be the best brunch-in recipe. These pizza pockets have it all: plant protein, vitamins and minerals, greens, cheese, and so much flavor! I'm guilty of eating these in the car when I'm running late to a meeting, and spilling hollandaise all over myself. Considering the fact that I'm always late, these pizza pockets have saved me more times than I can count. Make one or two batches on the weekend and just quickly heat them on a pan for the most epic and complete breakfast.

THE GOODS

Dough:

2 cups (480 ml) No-Strain Almond Milk (page 42)
1 (0.25-ounce [7 g]) packet active dry yeast
2 tablespoons (20 g) coconut sugar
¼ cup (60 ml) olive oil, plus more for cooking
¾ teaspoon salt
¾ teaspoon garlic powder
3⅓ cups (470 g) whole wheat or spelt flour; for GF, use 4 cups (540 g) + ¼ cup (35 g) 1-to-1 gluten-free baking flour

Tofu Scramble:

1 teaspoon olive oil
4 scallions, sliced, ends removed
3 garlic cloves, peeled and minced
½ teaspoon salt
1 (14-ounce [400 g]) block firm tofu, drained
1 teaspoon ground turmeric
¼ teaspoon freshly ground black pepper
½ teaspoon black salt
1 cup (30 g) stemmed and chopped kale
1 batch Muenster (page 100)
1 batch Hollandaise (page 125)

cashew-free

gluten-free optional

THE METHOD

① *First up, get your dough rising:* Microwave the almond milk in a microwave-safe bowl for 90 seconds, or until it reaches 105°F (41°C). It should be hot to the touch but not so hot that you can't touch it. Combine the active dry yeast, coconut sugar, and hot milk in a stand mixer fitted with a hook attachment, or a medium-size bowl. Let sit for about 10 minutes. Then, there should be a beginning layer of foam over the top of the milk; this is the sign that the yeast has

recipe continues →

activated. Turn on the mixer to medium speed or begin to mix with a fork. Add 2 tablespoons (30 ml) of the olive oil, and the salt and garlic powder, then mix for 30 seconds. Next, add the flour, 1 cup (140 g) at a time, while mixing, until you get a sticky but firm dough. Knead five to eight more times once all the flour is added to get a smooth dough. Coat a medium-size bowl with the remaining 2 tablespoons (30 ml) of the olive oil. Transfer the dough to the bowl, cover with a clean, damp kitchen towel, and let rise for at least an hour, or until it doubles in size.

② ***While the dough rises, make the tofu scramble:*** Combine the olive oil, scallions, garlic, and salt in a medium-size skillet over medium heat. Sauté for about 2 minutes, or until the garlic starts to brown. Add the tofu by crumbling it into the pan with your fingers. Add the rest of the topping ingredients and sauté for 5 more minutes, or until the tofu starts to lightly brown. Remove from the heat and set aside.

③ Preheat the oven to 200°F (93°C) when your dough is nearly done rising. After the dough has risen, dump it onto a clean cutting board, and cut into eight equal-size pieces. Knead each piece of dough six or seven times until you create eight dough balls. Set them aside. If using gluten-free flour, you will need to sprinkle 1 to 2 tablespoons (7.5 to 15 g) of flour per dough ball onto the cutting board before rolling it into a ball. If using spelt flour, and your dough is not sticking, don't worry about sprinkling flour onto the cutting board because it will actually dry out the spelt dough balls. With a rolling pin, roll out each ball into a palm-size disk. Take a tablespoon or two (15 to 30 g) of Muenster cheese and place on the center of a disk, top with 3 tablespoons (85 g) of tofu scramble (you may need more or less, depending on the size of your dough disks), then pull the sides of the disk toward the center, almost like folding a wonton. Pull up all the sides around the center until all the filling is inside the dough, then grab the ends and twist a full rotation, pressing it down to seal it. If using gluten-free flour, you won't be able to do the final twist at the end, but just press it closed as best as possible. Gently roll with a rolling pin to flatten the dough just enough before the dough breaks, or you can use your palm instead of the rolling pin. Repeat the process until you have made all your pizza pockets.

④ Heat a cast-iron griddle over medium heat. Then add 1 to 2 tablespoons (15 to 30 ml) of olive oil and place a pizza pocket on the griddle. Cook the first side for 2 to 3 minutes, or until a crust has created and started to turn golden brown. Optionally, brush the top with oil before you flip and cook the other side for 2 to 3 minutes. When both sides are golden brown, remove and keep warm in the preheated oven until it's time to serve. Serve hot with a generous drizzle of hollandaise. Store any extras in an airtight container for 5 days in the fridge or freezer. Reheat by searing on a cast-iron griddle or in a sauté pan for 1 minute per side.

cashew-free

gluten-free optional

Mini RED PEPPER QUICHES with Olive Oil Oat Crust

makes 12 mini quiches

These mini quiches are made with good-for-you ingredients that will truly get your day started in the absolute best way. The olive oil oat crust is the best GF alternative and is the most delicious vessel for these bites of heaven. Garbanzo (chickpea) flour is used here for a clean, high-protein egg replacement. And finally, these are filled with Pourable Mozzarella (page 88) that bakes like a dream inside the batter, making these cheese filled and ready for your next brunch, baby shower, or tailgate. Or, let's be real, you can just meal prep these to take the idea of thriving all week to the next level.

THE GOODS

Olive Oil Oat Crust:

2 cups (180 g) rolled oats or oat flour
1 teaspoon salt
¼ cup (60 ml) olive oil
¼ cup (60 ml) water

Quiche Filling:

1¾ cups (190 g) garbanzo (chickpea) flour
1 teaspoon black salt
1 teaspoon baking soda
½ teaspoon freshly ground black pepper
¾ teaspoon ground turmeric
1 teaspoon garlic powder
½ teaspoon salt
2¼ cups (540 ml) unsweetened plant-based milk or water
2 teaspoons freshly squeezed lemon juice
3 scallions, sliced
1 cup (60 g) shaved broccoli tops
1 cup (185 g) small-chopped jarred roasted red peppers
½ cup (120 ml) Pourable Mozzarella (page 88)

nut-free optional

gluten-free

soy-free optional

THE METHOD

① *Make the crust:* If using rolled oats, place the oats in a *dry* food processor or blender and process on high speed for about 45 seconds, or until it has the consistency of flour. If using store-bought oat flour, omit this step. Transfer the flour to a bowl, add the salt, olive oil, and water, and mix with a fork until the mixture has a doughlike consistency. Line a standard

recipe continues →

twelve-well muffin pan with paper liners or have ready four 4-inch round springform pans. Evenly press 2 to 3 tablespoons (16 to 24 g) of the dough on the bottom of each muffin well or springform pan. Set aside.

② Preheat the oven to 350°F (177°C). Combine the garbanzo flour, black salt, baking soda, black pepper, turmeric, garlic powder, and salt in a bowl and mix with a fork. Slowly pour in the plant-based milk while stirring. Add the lemon juice, scallions, broccoli, and roasted red peppers. Mix well and set aside for 5 to 10 minutes, to help the batter set.

③ Pour the batter atop the dough in your muffin wells or springform pans, filling three-quarters of the way full (the quiches will rise and overflow if there's too much). Place the mozzarella in a squeeze bottle, then puncture the center of each portion of filling with the squirt bottle nozzle and squeeze the bottle for 1 second to make a cheesy center. Bake the muffin-size quiches for 20 to 23 minutes; the springform quiches, for 30 to 34 minutes. You'll know they're done when you shake the pan slightly and the quiches stay firm, don't jiggle, and the top is golden brown. Remove from the oven and let cool for 15 to 20 minutes—this will allow them to set; otherwise, they can fall apart if you try to eat them straight from the oven. Enjoy warm or cold, or as a great meal prep for breakfast on the go. Store in an airtight container for 5 to 7 days.

nut-free optional

gluten-free

soy-free optional

Air-Fried RICOTTA BALLS with Ratatouille Sauce

serves 4

Romanticizing your life doesn't have to be complicated; in fact, it can start right here with this delicious dish best served up with friends and a baguette. This is one of those recipes that reminds you how much of an aphrodisiac cooking can be. The fresh tomatoes and fried little balls of ricotta cheese? And, oh yeah, did I mention the roasted garlic? This recipe is easily customizable to your preferences and allergies. Looking for a basic ricotta recipe? Use the one below; just omit the breadcrumbs and chia egg, and your next lasagna will be one for the books.

THE GOODS

Ratatouille Sauce:

½ small eggplant, sliced into ¼-inch rounds
2 teaspoons salt
1 medium-size zucchini, thinly sliced
1 red bell pepper, seeded and thinly sliced
1 medium-size onion, peeled and sliced
1½ cups (215 g) cherry tomatoes
Leaves from 1 sprig rosemary
1 teaspoon dried thyme
1 teaspoon dried oregano
½ teaspoon ground white pepper
2 teaspoons olive oil
Zest and juice of 1 lemon
1 garlic bulb, top removed

Almond Ricotta Balls (Soy-Free):

1½ cups (160 g) blanched almonds
2 tablespoons (30 ml) freshly squeezed lemon juice
1 teaspoon salt
3 garlic cloves, peeled
½ cup (120 ml) unsweetened plant-based milk of choice
¼ cup (20 g) chopped fresh basil
¾ cup (115 g) vegan breadcrumbs (GF if needed)
1 chia egg (1 tablespoon [7 g] ground chia seeds + 2½ tablespoons [37.5 ml] water)

Creamy Protein Ricotta Balls (Nut-Free):

1 (14-ounce [400 g]) block firm tofu, drained and patted dry
1¼ teaspoons salt
2 tablespoons (10 g) nutritional yeast
2 tablespoons (30 ml) freshly squeezed lemon juice
1 teaspoon garlic powder
¼ cup (20 g) chopped fresh basil
¾ cup (115 g) vegan breadcrumbs (GF if needed)
1 chia egg (1 tablespoon [7 g] ground chia seeds + 2½ tablespoons [37.5 ml] water)

recipe and ingredients continues →

nut-free optional

gluten-free optional

soy-free optional

grain-free

For Garnish:
Fresh basil leaves
Lemon zest

THE METHOD

① *Make the ratatouille sauce:* Preheat the oven to 400°F (205°C). Place the sliced eggplant on a plate or a baking pan, sprinkle 1 teaspoon of the salt onto the slices, and let sit for 15 to 20 minutes until they begin to sweat. Once the eggplant has sweated, use a towel to wipe the water from the eggplant. Combine the eggplant, zucchini, bell pepper, onion, cherry tomatoes, rosemary, thyme, oregano, white pepper, remaining teaspoon of salt, and 1 teaspoon of the olive oil in a bowl and stir until everything is fully mixed. Now, drizzle your lemon juice and sprinkle the lemon zest over the veggies and stir again. Pour the mixture into a single layer on a large baking sheet. Place your garlic bulb, cut side up, in a corner of the baking sheet. Pour the other teaspoon of olive oil over the exposed side of the garlic bulb. Bake for 35 to 40 minutes, or until garlic is soft and fragrant and the veggies are starting to caramelize.

② Next, remove from the oven and carefully pour all the hot veggies, except the garlic bulb, into a high-powered blender. Squeeze the garlic cloves from the garlic bulb into your blender and blend on high speed for 30 seconds, or until fully mixed. Pour into a saucepan and cover with a lid to keep warm.

③ *Meanwhile, make your ricotta:* If you're making the almond ricotta, combine the blanched almonds, lemon juice, salt, garlic cloves, and plant-based milk in a high-powered blender, and blend on high speed for 2 to 3 minutes while using an accelerator stick, until you have a thick, delicious, and textured ricotta. If you're making the creamy protein ricotta instead, combine the tofu, salt, nutritional yeast, lemon juice, and garlic powder in a high-powered blender, and blend on high speed for 2 to 3 minutes, using the accelerator stick, until the ricotta is creamy. Transfer the ricotta cheese of your choice to a bowl, toss in the basil, breadcrumbs, and chia egg, and fold until fully mixed.

④ Preheat an air fryer to 400°F (205°C). Using a 1-inch ice cream scooper, scoop the ricotta into 1-inch balls and place in the air fryer. Air fry for 8 to 10 minutes. Alternatively, you can pop these in the oven, laid out on a large, parchment paper–lined baking sheet, for about 20 minutes. Once the cheese balls have a crispy outer shell, remove them from the air fryer or oven, transfer to a bowl, and set aside.

⑤ When the sauce is ready and the cheese balls are crispy, it's time to serve. Spoon a generous amount of ratatouille sauce onto a few single-serving plates or a large platter, and then top with your desired amount of cheese balls. (No limit here!) Garnish with basil leaves and lemon zest. Serve immediately while still warm.

nut-free optional

gluten-free optional

soy-free optional

grain-free

Double TRUFFLE FRIES

serves 2 or 3, or 1

This recipe will help you lean into the finer things in life and the side of yourself that wants the cake, and to eat it too. These fries are baked, not fried, and are caramelized with coconut sugar, making them healthy yet so dang delicious.

THE GOODS

6 russet potatoes, washed, peeled, and julienned
2 tablespoons (30 ml) olive oil
1 teaspoon truffle salt
1 teaspoon dried dill
½ teaspoon ground white pepper
1 teaspoon coconut sugar (sub organic cane sugar for coconut allergy)
1 garlic bulb, top sliced off (for truffle sauce)

Truffle Sauce:
1 cup (240 ml) plain crema (page 129)
1 teaspoon lemon zest
1 tablespoon (15 ml) freshly squeezed lemon juice
½ teaspoon salt
1 tablespoon (15 ml) truffle oil, or ½ teaspoon truffle powder
¼ cup (5 g) minced fresh parsley

THE METHOD

① Preheat the oven to 400°F (205°C). Line a large baking sheet with parchment paper and set aside.

② Combine the potatoes, 1½ tablespoons (22.5 ml) of the olive oil, truffle salt, dried dill, white pepper, and coconut sugar in a large bowl, and toss until all the potato pieces are coated. Arrange them in a single layer on the prepared baking sheet; if they seem a little too crowded, you can divide them between two prepared baking sheets so they can evenly brown. Place the garlic bulb, cut side up, in the corner of the baking sheet, and drizzle the remaining 1½ teaspoons of olive oil over the top. Bake for 25 minutes, remove from the oven and stir, then pop back in for 20 to 25 more minutes, or until the potatoes are fork-tender and golden brown, and the garlic is soft and fragrant. You may need to pull the garlic out early, so keep an eye on it.

③ *Make the truffle sauce:* Place the crema in your high-powered blender. Squeeze out the roasted garlic cloves from their bulb into the blender, add the lemon zest and juice, salt, and truffle oil, and blend on high speed for 30 seconds. Add the parsley and pulse four to six times to incorporate without changing the color of the sauce to green. Transfer the sauce to a bowl and set aside.

④ Once the potatoes have become soft and slightly golden brown, remove from the oven and serve warm with the truffle sauce.

nut-free optional

gluten-free

soy-free optional

grain-free

Mozzarella Sage GARLIC ROLLS

makes 7 rolls

Nothing pairs with a cocktail quite like a cheesy garlic roll, and if you're ready to be the life of the party, these have to come with you. This is just another recipe to show how versatile the Pourable Mozzarella (page 88) can be; honestly, the limit for the amount of cheese you use does not exist here. It pairs the technique of making a cinnamon roll with the irresistible flavors of garlic, cheese, and sage. All the best worlds combined to make you, well, the life of the party.

THE GOODS

Garlic Knots:

1½ cups (360 ml) unsweetened plant-based milk of choice
1 tablespoon (10 g) coconut sugar (sub cane sugar for coconut allergy)
1 (0.25-ounce [7 g]) packet active dry yeast
1 teaspoon garlic powder
1 teaspoon salt
3 cups (420 g) spelt, all-purpose, or whole wheat flour, plus more for dusting, if needed
1 teaspoon olive oil
3 cups (720 ml) Pourable Mozzarella (page 88)

Garlic Sage Butter:

¼ cup (60 ml) melted salted butter (see the Butter Block, page 122)
1 shallot, peeled and minced
1 teaspoon salt
5 garlic cloves, peeled and minced
9 fresh sage leaves, minced

THE METHOD

① *Make the garlic knots:* Heat the plant-based milk in a saucepan to about 105°F (41°C), hot to the touch but not so hot that it will burn your finger. Then, remove from the heat and pour, along with the coconut sugar and active dry yeast, into a large bowl or stand mixer fitted with the dough hook attachment. Let the mixture sit for 10 minutes until the yeast blooms and creates a foam on the top of the milk. Next, add the garlic powder and salt, and then the spelt flour, 1 cup (140 g) at a time, on a low kneading setting or by mixing with a fork and then switching to your hands. If you find that you are getting a nice tacky yet solid dough before you use all the flour, use your best judgment as to how much you need.

② Knead the dough about ten more times until you have a smooth and bouncy dough ball. Oil a separate bowl with the olive oil, cover with a clean, damp cloth, and let rise for an hour.

③ *Make the garlic sage butter:* Heat the butter in a saucepan over medium-low heat until it melts, for about 90 seconds. Once it starts to turn golden brown and bubble, add the shallot and salt,

recipe continues →

soy-free

and sauté for 1 minute. Next, toss in the garlic and sage leaves, and sauté for another 2 to 3 minutes over medium-low heat. Remove from the heat.

④ Your dough should have doubled in size now. Preheat the oven to 400°F (205°C). Transfer the dough to a large, clean surface. It shouldn't be sticking because of the oil, but if the dough is still a bit sticky, dust some flour onto your work surface. With a rolling pin, roll out the dough ball into a rectangle about 9 x 10 inches, making sure the dough stays at least ½ inch thick.

⑤ Once you have your rectangle, brush the garlic sage butter over the top of the dough. Then, just as you would for cinnamon rolls, roll up your dough lengthwise, like a hot dog, trapping the butter inside. Using a pizza cutter, cut seven 2-inch rolls. Next, pour 1 cup (240 ml) of the mozzarella into a 9-inch pie pan or oven-safe ceramic skillet. Add the rolls, placing each cut side up. Once all the knots are tucked inside the pan, let them rise for another 15 minutes. After the final rise, pour the rest of the mozzarella over the top, then bake for 20 to 25 minutes, or until the cheese and rolls have formed a crust and are golden on the top. For the final 2 minutes, broil on HIGH to brown the top. Remove from the oven and let cool for 1 to 2 minutes.

⑥ Serve with red pepper flakes, flaky sea salt, and your favorite dipping sauce, such as Bai's Special Sauce (page 129). These are best enjoyed right out of the oven but will keep for 2 to 3 days in the fridge.

soy-free

Parmesan POLENTA FRIES with Tarragon Dijon Sauce

makes 18 to 20 fries

Polenta and tarragon are two of my absolute favorite ingredients, and honestly don't get the hype they deserve. These polenta fries are perfectly savory while being crispy on the outside and soft on the inside. They are a little bit of a labor of love but are absolutely the best party food and are so easy to make ahead of time and reheat when the time is right. Paired with the most delicious, velvety sauce, they will be sure to be on your party roster over and over again.

THE GOODS

Polenta:

1½ cups (360 ml) veggie broth
2 cups (480 ml) unsweetened plant-based milk
1 teaspoon salt
1 cup (160 g) polenta

Parmesan Crust:

→ (To make this nut-free, just replace the walnuts with the same amount of vegan, GF breadcrumbs)
1 cup (110 g) walnuts
½ cup (65 g) hemp seeds
1 tablespoon (5 g) nutritional yeast
½ teaspoon salt
¾ cup (75 g) vegan, gluten-free breadcrumbs
½ cup (60 g) tapioca starch
1 cup (240 ml) unsweetened plant-based milk

Dijon Sun-Dried Tomato Sauce:

1 cup (130 g) hemp seeds
¼ cup (60 g) sun-dried tomatoes
1 tablespoon (15 g) Dijon mustard
1½ teaspoons salt
½ teaspoon freshly ground black pepper
2 tablespoons (30 ml) freshly squeezed lemon juice
1¼ cups (300 ml) unsweetened plant-based milk
1 tablespoon (3 g) chopped tarragon, plus more for garnish
Lemon wedges to garnish

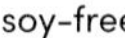

nut-free option gluten-free soy-free oil-free

THE METHOD

① *Make the polenta:* Line a 9 x 9-inch baking dish with parchment paper. To get the parchment more flexible, crinkle it into a tiny little ball and then uncrinkle it. Set aside.

② Combine the veggie broth, plant-based milk, and salt in a 5-quart pot and bring to a boil. Then add the polenta and cook over medium-low heat for about 10 minutes while whisking. Pour the polenta into the prepared baking dish, smooth out the top, and let

recipe continues →

cool on the countertop for about 30 minutes. Place in the fridge for about 30 more minutes, to set.

③ ***Meanwhile, make the Parmesan crust:*** Combine the walnuts, hemp seeds, nutritional yeast, salt, and breadcrumbs in a *dry* blender or food processor, then blend or process on high speed for 3 to 5 seconds, or until they have the consistency of a grainy powder. If there are some clumps, it's okay; just crush them. Pour the mixture into a large shallow bowl. Place the tapioca starch in another shallow bowl, and the plant-based milk in a third shallow bowl. Set aside.

④ Preheat your oven to 450°F (232°C), and line a large baking sheet with parchment paper. Remove the polenta block from the fridge and cut into eighteen to twenty 3-inch rectangles. These are your fries.

⑤ Now, it's time to bread these baddies! In a conveyor-belt formation, working one by one, coat each fry in tapioca starch, pat off any excess flour, then dip it in the plant-based milk and coat with the Parmesan crumb mixture. Place the finished fry on the prepared baking sheet. Repeat with all the fries. I find it helpful to use one hand for dry coating and the other for wet. Make sure there's just enough space between each fry so that the hot air from the oven can pass through them. Bake for 20 minutes, and then turn them all over so they can evenly brown. Bake for another 10 minutes.

⑥ ***Make the sauce:*** Combine all the sauce ingredients in a high-powered blender, and blend for about 20 seconds, or until smooth. Pour the sauce into a serving bowl. Set aside.

⑦ Once the fries are done, use a spatula to remove them from the pan and place them on a serving tray along with the sauce. I like to garnish with extra minced tarragon and a lemon wedge. These are best enjoyed immediately but can be reheated within 5 to 7 days after storing in an airtight container in the fridge.

nut-free option

gluten-free

soy-free

oil-free

Sweet Pepper POPPERS

makes 26 to 30

Jalapeño poppers are usually reserved for football season, but this one is for all seasons. It's the vibe of jalapeño poppers without the stomachache and heartburn. I also love this recipe for a crowd because it's allergy-friendly and so tasty with the crispy corn chip topping. The sweet peppers make this recipe one of my favorites, but if you want to add a little spice to your life, you can throw a couple of jalapeños in there to keep the vibes hot and spicy.

THE GOODS

Chip Crumble:

3 cups (60 g) vegan tortilla chips
½ teaspoon garlic powder
½ teaspoon chili powder
½ teaspoon ground coriander

Poppers:

1 cup (140 g) hulled sunflower seeds
1 (15-ounce [425 g]) can white beans, drained and rinsed
½ cup (120 ml) unsweetened plant-based milk
1½ teaspoons salt
1 teaspoon garlic powder
1 tablespoon (5 g) nutritional yeast
1 tablespoon (15 ml) freshly squeezed lemon juice
1 tablespoon (15 ml) hot sauce
1 tablespoon (3 g) minced fresh chives
13 to 15 sweet mini peppers, cut in half and seeded

THE METHOD

① *Make the chip crumble:* Preheat the oven to 350°F (177°C). Combine all the chip crumble ingredients in a *dry* high-powered blender or food processor, and blend or process on high speed for about 15 seconds, or until you get an even crumb. Pour the crumble into a bowl and set aside.

② *Make the poppers:* Combine the sunflower seeds, white beans, plant-based milk, salt, garlic powder, nutritional yeast, lemon juice, hot sauce, and chives in the same blender or food processor. Blend or process on high speed for about 45 seconds, or until you have a smooth mixture. Scoop about 1 tablespoon (15 ml) of the mixture into a pepper half and level off so you have a smooth surface. Carefully dip the side that's filled into the chip crumble, to evenly coat that side of the popper. Repeat with all the peppers. Bake for 10 to 15 minutes, or until the crumble topping is golden brown and the peppers are semisoft. Enjoy immediately with a beer and your bestie.

nut-free

gluten-free

soy-free

oil-free

Gravlax DILL DIP

serves 3 or 4

In my previous life, I used to go to great lengths to get a New York–style bagel with an obnoxious amount of cream cheese and lox. It was a craving I would do anything to satisfy, and if I had a wild night, you better believe this was my breakfast. This dip takes the breakfast lox bagel and brings it right into happy hour. It serves so well with toasted and buttered bread and will satisfy that craving for lox anytime of the day.

THE GOODS

1 teaspoon olive oil
1 small shallot, peeled and minced
4 garlic cloves, peeled and sliced
½ teaspoon salt
1 large carrot, peeled into ribbons
1 tablespoon (15 ml) tamari
1½ teaspoons (7.5 ml) agave nectar
1 teaspoon smoked paprika
1 teaspoon kelp flakes
1 batch crema of choice (page 129); I prefer the Indulgent Queen
¼ cup (3 g) chopped fresh dill
2 tablespoons (30 ml) freshly squeezed lemon juice

THE METHOD

Heat a medium-size sauté pan or cast-iron skillet over medium-high heat. Add the olive oil and shallot, and sauté for 1 to 2 minutes, or until the shallot becomes fragrant. Lower the heat to medium, then add the garlic and salt. After cooking the garlic for 30 seconds, toss in the carrot ribbons and cook for 2 minutes. Pour in the tamari and agave, and cook for 1 minute. Add the paprika and kelp, and cook, stirring frequently, for 1 minute more. Turn the heat down to low and add the crema, dill, and lemon juice. Simmer, stirring, for 2 to 3 more minutes, or until it turns a light, orangey salmon color. Remove from the heat and let cool for 5 minutes before transferring to a bowl and enjoying with bread, crackers, or chips. Store the leftovers in an airtight container for 5 to 7 days.

nut-free optional

gluten-free

grain-free

The Compound BUTTER SERIES

makes about 2 cups

setting time: 1 hour

As a French-trained chef, I couldn't write a book about dairy without including some of my favorite compound butters. A compound butter is basically a butter packed with flavor and can be used to elevate any dish. My personal favorite is to just simply toast a baguette and top it with one of these butters, but you can add them to potatoes or soup, use as a base for a sauce, or serve them with breakfast. There's something here for everyone, and trust me when I say that the juice is worth the squeeze with this one.

→ START WITH A BASE

The Butter Block (page 122), salted or unsalted per your choice of the following flavors

→ CHOOSE YOUR FLAVORS

Roasted Garlic Rosemary

THE GOODS

1 garlic bulb, top sliced off
1½ teaspoons (7.5 ml) olive oil
Pinch of salt
1 salted Butter Block (page 122)
2 tablespoons (4 g) fresh rosemary, minced

THE METHOD

Preheat an oven or air fryer to 350°F (177°C). Place the garlic bulb, cut side up, in a small oven-safe bowl or baking dish, and sprinkle with the olive oil and salt. Roast for 20 minutes, or until the garlic is soft. Remove from the oven and let cool completely. While the garlic cools, remove the Butter Block from the fridge so it can soften for 10 to 15 minutes. Then, place the Butter Block in a stand mixer fitted with a paddle attachment, or in a bowl, add the rosemary, and squeeze the garlic out of the bulb onto the butter. Mix until everything is combined, for about 45 seconds, or if by hand, with a spatula; it depends on how strong you are . . . you got this! Scoop into a Glasslock container and let set for about an hour in the fridge. Best used within 10 to 12 days.

gluten-free

soy-free

recipes continue →

Maple Bacon

THE GOODS

1 medium-size carrot
1 tablespoon (15 ml) liquid aminos
1 tablespoon (15 ml) pure maple syrup
1 teaspoon smoked paprika
Salted Butter Block (page 122)

THE METHOD

Using a peeler, "ribbon" the carrot by consistently peeling one side of the carrot in one direction. Once you have a bunch of ribbons, place them on a cutting board and small chop. Transfer the chopped carrots to a bowl along with the liquid aminos, maple syrup, and smoked paprika. Stir, then let marinate for 30 minutes. Heat a medium-size cast-iron skillet over medium heat. Then put in the carrots, sautéing until they become soft, caramelized, and browned, for about 5 minutes, periodically adding the leftover marinade while cooking, to deglaze the pan, if needed, and prevent burning. Remove from the heat and set aside to cool. Next, pull the butter out of the fridge to soften for 10 to 15 minutes. Then, combine the butter and the carrots in a stand mixer fitted with a paddle attachment, or in a bowl. Mix until everything is well blended, for about 45 seconds, or if mixing by hand, use a spatula. Scoop into a Glasslock container and let set for about an hour in the fridge. Best used within 10 to 12 days.

Brown Butter Fig

THE GOODS

Unsalted Butter Block (page 122)
2 tablespoons (30 ml) pure maple syrup
3 tablespoons (30 g) coconut sugar (sub cane sugar for coconut allergy)
5 large figs, stemmed and diced

THE METHOD

Remove the butter from the fridge so it can soften for 10 to 15 minutes. Combine the maple syrup, coconut sugar, and figs in a saucepan. Cook over medium-low heat, stirring with a rubber spatula, for 5 minutes, or until the figs soften and the coconut sugar dissolves. Remove from the heat and set aside for 10 to 15 minutes, or until cool. Combine the butter and the fig mixture in a stand mixer fitted with a paddle attachment, or in a bowl with a spatula. Mix until everything is combined, for about 45 seconds. Scoop into a Glasslock container and let set for about an hour in the fridge. Best used within 10 to 12 days.

gluten-free

soy-free

Chili Crunch

THE GOODS

Unsalted Butter Block (page 122)
1½ teaspoons salt
1 tablespoon (2 g) minced fresh basil
4 teaspoons (60 g) garlic chili crunch
1 tablespoon (5 g) black sesame seeds
1 tablespoon (15 ml) freshly squeezed lemon juice

THE METHOD

First, remove the butter from the fridge and let it sit for 10 to 15 minutes to soften. Then, combine the butter, salt, basil, garlic chili crunch, black sesame seeds, and lemon juice in a stand mixer fitted with a paddle attachment, or in a bowl with a spatula, and whip for 45 seconds. Scoop into a Glasslock container and store in the fridge for 10 to 12 days. Use it on your favorite savory dishes or sandwiches.

gluten-free

soy-free

Fried Chèvre PEACH SALAD with White Balsamic

serves 4 or 5

During my time as a single gal living in San Francisco, I would visit this little French bistro and order myself a glass of Champagne and a fried goat cheese salad similar to this one. Although this recipe is made to share with friends, it is an easy reminder that all you need to be happy in this life is yourself, a good vibe, and an incredible meal. To make this successfully, make sure the chèvre log is extra cold, the last thing to pull out of the fridge before you bread and fry it. If you live in a hot climate, freeze the chèvre for twenty minutes before slicing and frying.

THE GOODS

Fried Chèvre:

- ⅓ cup (50 g) tapioca starch or cornstarch
- 1 cup (240 ml) unsweetened plant-based milk
- 2½ cups (250 g) vegan breadcrumbs (GF if needed)
- Olive oil, for frying
- ½ batch (8 ounces) Chèvre Log (page 103), cut into thin slices

Peach Salad:

- 4 cups (140 g) arugula
- 3 to 4 heirloom tomatoes, sliced
- 2 to 3 peaches, pitted and sliced
- 2 tablespoons (30 ml) white balsamic vinegar
- 2 tablespoons (30 ml) organic olive oil
- 2 tablespoons (30 ml) freshly squeezed lemon juice
- ¼ cup (25 g) vegan breadcrumbs (GF if needed)
- Freshly ground black pepper
- Lemon zest

THE METHOD

① *Make the fried chèvre:* Next to your stovetop, line up three shallow bowls, one for each of the tapioca starch, plant-based milk, and breadcrumbs. Set aside a clean plate (for the fried cheese). Heat a glug of olive oil in a nonstick or cast-iron skillet over medium-low heat. In a conveyor-belt fashion, working a few slices of cheese at a time, dip a slice of goat cheese into the tapioca starch to coat it,

recipe continues →

cashew-free

gluten-free optional

grain-free

tap off any extra starch, and then place it in the plant-based milk, and finally, dip it into the breadcrumbs until coated. Place the slice on the heated pan. Cook on each side for 30 to 45 seconds until lightly golden brown. Don't overcook them because you want these to hold their shape and they will melt quickly. Remove from the heat and place each fried goat cheese slice directly on the nearby clean plate.

② ***Make your peach salad:*** Spread the arugula evenly over a large serving plate. Top with the tomato and peach slices, then carefully place a few fried cheese slices on top. Finish with a drizzle of the white balsamic, olive oil, and lemon juice. Shake the breadcrumbs on top for an added crunch, plus a sprinkle of pepper and lemon zest. Enjoy immediately with a glass of Champagne while the cheese is still warm.

cashew-free

gluten-free optional

grain-free

Crab POTATO PANCAKES with Tartar Sauce

makes 12; serves 6

My Polish family leans hard into potato pancakes for holidays and for family gatherings. I also used to be obsessed with crab cakes for happy hours. So, naturally, I needed to combine the two to make the epic appetizer that I'm calling a crab potato pancake. The hearts of palm are a perfect sub for the crab and work perfectly with the starch in the potatoes for the best texture ever. Serve these with Tartar Sauce (page 145) to bring old traditions to new heights.

THE GOODS

6 small russet potatoes, washed and peeled
1 (14-ounce [400 g]) can hearts of palm, drained, rinsed, and diced
1 onion, peeled and shredded
2 chia eggs (2 tablespoons [15 g] ground chia seeds + ¼ cup [60 ml] water)
1 tablespoon (15 ml) olive oil, plus more for frying
1 teaspoon granulated garlic
1 teaspoon paprika
1 teaspoon ground kelp flakes
1 teaspoon salt
½ teaspoon freshly ground black pepper
3 tablespoons (30 g) cassava flour or oat flour
1 to 2 tablespoons (15 to 30 ml) avocado oil (optional if air-frying)
Tartar Sauce (page 145)
Lemon wedges

THE METHOD

① Pass the russet potatoes through a shredder attachment on a food processor. Place the shredded potatoes in a large colander, then, with clean hands, press down and squeeze out as much water as possible for 1 to 2 minutes. This step is important. Place the squeezed potatoes in a bowl along with the hearts of palm and onion, and mix well with a fork. Now, create the chia eggs in a small bowl, and let sit for 60 seconds to set. Add the chia eggs, olive oil,

recipe continues →

nut-free

gluten-free

soy-free

grain-free optional

garlic, paprika, kelp flakes, salt, and pepper. Mix well with a fork to incorporate all the ingredients. Finally, sprinkle the cassava flour over the top and mix well.

② Heat a regular or cast-iron skillet over medium heat. While the pan heats, scoop out ½ cup (70 g) of the potato mixture and create a hockey puck shape with your hands, then flatten it to create a pancake. Pour a dash of avocado oil into the pan, then fry the potato pancakes in batches. Cook for 4 to 7 minutes on each side. The timing will vary depending on how thick your pan is. Top up the oil, if needed, until all the latkes are cooked. If you want to use less oil, you can air fry at 400°F (205°C) for 6 minutes on each side (flip halfway through).

③ To keep the latkes warm while you're frying, you can set the oven to 200°F (93°C) and place them on a baking sheet as they finish frying. Serve with tartar sauce and lemon wedges. Best enjoyed immediately or within 3 days of making. Store leftovers in an airtight container in the fridge.

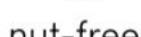
nut-free

gluten-free

soy-free

grain-free optional

Buffalo CHICK'N DIP

serves 2 or 3

This recipe is dedicated to my husband, the guy that got me to break up with dairy in the first place. He will eat pretty much anything smothered in Buffalo sauce, so naturally we had to make this crowd-pleasing dip 100 percent dairy-free. I used the Protein Hero Crema (page 129) and pinto beans, so that although you're not getting protein from chicken, you don't need to worry about not hitting your protein goals. This one is a crowd-pleaser, a husband pleaser, and most important, even more epic on a hoagie.

THE GOODS

- 2 (16-ounce [450 g]) cans green jackfruit, drained and rinsed
- 1 teaspoon olive oil
- 1 onion, peeled and sliced
- 1 teaspoon salt
- 4 garlic cloves, peeled and sliced
- 1 teaspoon ground cumin
- 2 teaspoons dried oregano
- 1 (15.5-ounce [440-g]) can pinto beans, drained and rinsed
- 1 cup (240 ml) dairy-free Buffalo sauce
- 1 cup (240 ml) Protein Hero Crema (page 129)
- 1 teaspoon smoked paprika

THE METHOD

① First, place the jackfruit in a colander and begin to squeeze the water out of it. When you begin to get a shredded chicken consistency, transfer it to a bowl and set aside, next to your stovetop.

② Combine the olive oil, onion, and salt in a large sauté pan over medium-high heat. Cook the onion for 2 minutes, or until fragrant and just starting to turn golden and translucent. Next, add the garlic and sauté for 1 minute. Toss in the prepped jackfruit and sauté for 2 to 3 minutes more. Sprinkle in the cumin and oregano, then toast the spices for 1 to 2 minutes. Use a splash of water, if needed to deglaze the pan at any point, to prevent overcooking. Toss in the pinto beans and Buffalo sauce, and cook, stirring and breaking up any larger jackfruit pieces with your spatula, for another 1 to 2 minutes.

③ Turn the heat down to medium-low and add the Protein Hero Crema and paprika. Cook, stirring, for another 4 minutes, or until fully combined. Remove from the heat, cover, and serve immediately. Best served with vegan bread, chips, crackers, etc. Store leftovers in the refrigerator. Best used within 5 days.

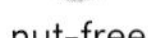

nut-free

gluten-free

grain-free

WHIPPED FETA with Tomato Garlic Confit

serves 4 or 5

Grab a bottle of sauvignon blanc, a rustic loaf of sourdough, call your bestie, and dive into this epic appetizer meant for a crowd but perfect for two to indulge in. I love a whipped feta and also anything that is smothered in garlic. We use twenty cloves of garlic in this recipe, and no, that's not a typo. Make the feta ahead of time, but be sure to make the garlic confit when ready to serve because we want it warm, bubbly, and freshly made.

THE GOODS

Tomato Confit:

2 cups (280 g) cherry tomatoes
20 garlic cloves, peeled
¾ cup (180 ml) olive oil
4 sprigs oregano
4 sprigs thyme
3 sprigs rosemary
1 teaspoon flaky sea salt

Whipped Feta:

1 (14-ounce [400 g]) block firm tofu
3 tablespoons (45 ml) freshly squeezed lemon juice
2 tablespoons (40 g) miso paste
1 tablespoon (15 ml) white balsamic vinegar
¼ cup (60 ml) unsweetened coconut yogurt or cashew yogurt
1 teaspoon salt

THE METHOD

① *Make the tomato confit:* Preheat the oven to 400°F (205°C). Arrange the cherry tomatoes, garlic cloves, olive oil, and oregano, thyme, and rosemary sprigs on a baking sheet or in a baking dish, then sprinkle with the flaky sea salt. Bake for 30 minutes, or until the tomato skins are soft and the garlic is golden brown.

② *Make the whipped feta:* Combine all the ingredients for the whipped feta in a high-powered blender. Blend on high speed for 60 seconds, or until everything is fully smooth. Set aside in the blender.

③ When the tomatoes are soft and golden brown, remove the veggies from the oven. Pour the whipped feta from the blender into the center of a rimmed, medium-size serving plate. Using a flat-head spatula, scoop the tomato confit from the hot baking sheet, and garnish the whipped feta with the confit. Place the herb sprigs on the side, remove some leaves, and use those for garnish. Serve warm. Keep the leftovers in an airtight container for 3 to 4 days.

nut-free

gluten-free

grain-free

San Diego LOBSTA' ROLL

makes 3 or 4 sandwiches

There's a Maine lobster roll, a Connecticut lobster roll, and today I'd like to introduce you to the San Diego Lobsta' Roll. This sandwich is part of a family but also is very much one-of-a-kind. Lobster rolls are known for being dripped in butter, on a hot hoagie, and best enjoyed by the ocean. Not only is this lobster roll more sustainable than its East Coast counterparts, but it's got a San Diego twist by being smothered in the chorizo-inspired Bai's Special Sauce (page 129). King oyster mushrooms are used here because, once you sear them on a cast iron with butter and garlic, they take on a whole new lobster vibe.

THE GOODS

- 18 ounces (510 g) king oyster mushrooms
- 2 tablespoons (30 g) salted vegan butter (see the Butter Block, page 122)
- 1 teaspoon salt
- 4 garlic cloves, minced
- 1 (14-ounce [400 g]) can hearts of palm, drained, rinsed, and chopped small
- 1 teaspoon kelp flakes
- ½ teaspoon paprika, plus more for garnish
- 2 celery ribs, thinly sliced
- ½ cup (120 ml) Bai's Special Sauce (page 129), plus more for hoagies
- ¼ cup (10 g) chopped fresh parsley, plus more for garnish
- 3 or 4 hoagie rolls (GF if needed), sliced sandwich style

THE METHOD

① Cut the mushrooms in half lengthwise, then cut into 2-inch pieces diagonally (think: lobster claws) and set aside. Heat a large cast-iron skillet over medium-high heat. Then, dry sauté the mushrooms for 3 to 4 minutes, using a potato masher or something similar to smash them every 30 seconds. This will release the water and help the mushrooms brown and change shape. Once the mushrooms are starting to

recipe continues →

nut-free

gluten-free optional

soy-free

soften, add the butter and salt, and toss with the mushrooms. When the butter is melted, cook for 4 to 5 minutes, or until the mushrooms are starting to develop golden-brown edges. Next, toss in the garlic cloves and hearts of palm, and sauté for 2 to 3 minutes. Sprinkle with the kelp flakes and paprika, sauté for 1 to 2 minutes, then remove from the heat.

② Transfer the mushroom mixture to a large bowl along with the celery, Bai's Special Sauce, and parsley, and stir until fully mixed. Taste for salt. Set aside.

③ Toast your hoagie rolls, and to serve, add a generous amount of Bai's Special Sauce and a scoop or two of the lobster to each roll, then garnish with paprika and parsley. Enjoy warm!

nut-free

gluten-free optional

soy-free

Neapolitan Vodka CAPRESE PIZZA

makes two 12-inch pizzas or one 15-inch GF pizza

You can't successfully break up with dairy and feel like a boss in the kitchen without having a really solid pizza under your belt. For me, a pizza is just as much about the crust and the sauce as it is about the cheese. Neapolitan-style pizzas are my favorite because the crust is thin and crispy, yet chewy, and absolutely not something you leave behind. This whole wheat Neapolitan crust with a two-hour rise time makes this doable for the average person but still *incredible* for a homemade pizza. To give the crust a little extra love and attention, after it rises, put it in an airtight bag in the fridge to ferment overnight, to have truly the best crust of your life. This recipe combines a few of my favorites throughout the book. If you want the most incredible pizza, incorporate them all. If you're short on time, pick and choose what you want to top this one with.

THE GOODS

Herbed Whole Wheat Crust:

3 cups (435 g) whole wheat flour, or 3 cups (450 g) 1-to-1 gluten-free baking flour
1 (0.25-ounce [7 g]) packet active dry yeast
1½ teaspoons salt
1 tablespoon (3 g) minced fresh rosemary
1 teaspoon dried basil
1 teaspoon dried thyme
3 tablespoons (45 ml) olive oil
1½ cups (360 ml) warm water, or for GF, 1¼ cups (300 ml) warm water
2 tablespoons (20 g) cornmeal, plus more if needed

Pizza Toppings:

½ cup (120 ml) Vodka Sauce (page 135, made without pasta water) per whole wheat pizza, or ¾ cup for a single GF pizza
½ cup (70 g) cherry tomatoes, sliced, per whole wheat pizza, or 1 cup (140 g) for a single GF pizza
3 or 4 Mozzarella Balls (page 109), per whole wheat pizza, or 6 to 8 for a single GF pizza
5 to 7 fresh basil leaves
Truffle Sauce (page 220, optional)

Crust Coating:

Olive oil, for brushing
Dried basil
Flaky sea salt
Granulated garlic

THE METHOD

① *Make the dough:* Combine the flour, active dry yeast, and salt in a stand mixer fitted with a hook attachment or in a large bowl. Stir with a fork until everything is mixed. Then, add

recipe continues →

gluten-free optional

the fresh and dried herbs and stir until fully mixed. Pour in 2 tablespoons (30 ml) of the olive oil and ¼ cup (60 ml) of the water at a time while forming the pizza dough on a low setting in the stand mixer or by mixing by hand. Knead eight to nine times into a dough ball once the dough has formed. It will be sticky. Once the dough ball is semisoft and round, oil a clean bowl with the remaining tablespoon (15 ml) of olive oil, and transfer the dough to that bowl. Cover with a clean, damp kitchen towel and let sit out at room temperature for 2 hours.

② ***For a whole wheat crust (makes 2):*** After 2 hours, the dough should have doubled in size. Punch the dough lightly with your fist, and then dump it onto a clean cutting board. Cut the dough in half and knead each half three or four times while rolling each into a dough ball on your cutting board. Place the balls on a plate, cover with the same damp kitchen towel (redampen it if you need to), and let rise for 20 more minutes.

③ While waiting for the dough to rise, have ready your vodka sauce and mozzarella balls.

④ When the dough has risen, preheat the oven to 500°F (260°C). Sprinkle one 20-inch pizza pan with the cornmeal. With your hands, slowly pull the dough into a 10-inch-diameter pizza crust for each individual dough ball. Avoid using a rolling pin here; pull the dough while letting gravity do the work. Now, make a fist, place the dough around your fist, and let it fall over the sides. Alternatively, you can grab one side, hold it up, and wiggle it a little to let it drop closer to the cutting board. If you take it a little too far and you get holes in the dough, just knead it into a ball again, let rest for 10 minutes, and try again. Once you have two glorious 12- to 13-inch crusts, carefully transfer them to the cornmeal-dusted pan. Pour about ½ cup (120 ml) of the vodka sauce in the center, spread it around as a thin layer, then top with the halved cherry tomatoes and dollops of the mozzarella balls. Brush olive oil over the crust and then sprinkle on dried basil, flaky sea salt, and granulated garlic. Don't skip this step, as it really takes this pizza to the next level. Bake for 8 minutes, or until the edges are golden brown. Garnish with the fresh basil leaves after you pull it from the oven. Let cool for 5 minutes before enjoying. Maybe even enjoy this pizza with my creamy truffle sauce if you're feeling the vibes.

For a GF crust: Preheat the oven to 500°F (260°C). Line a 20-inch pizza pan with parchment paper. Dump the dough onto the prepared pan, and with a rolling pin, roll out into a 15-inch-diameter crust. Use your fingers to create a little lift for the crust and to smooth out the sides for an even circle. Pour about ¾ cup (180 ml) of the vodka sauce in the center, spread it around as a thin layer, then top with 1 cup (140 g) of cherry tomatoes and six to eight mozzarella balls. Brush olive oil over the crust and then sprinkle on dried basil, flaky sea salt, and granulated garlic. Don't skip this step, as it really takes this pizza to the next level. Bake for 14 to 16 minutes. Garnish with fresh basil leaves.

gluten-free optional

soy-free

8. The SWEETEST THING

IT'S THE FINAL CHAPTER, so I'm thinking that it's time we make this official. You are officially a dairy-free baddie. The breakup is over, and you're on to bigger and better things. Ice cream. Milkshakes. Flan. Tiramisu. Maybe you thought breaking up with dairy meant a life without treats. Not in the slightest. I'm here to show you the depth and real pleasure of a dairy-free life through the eyes of dessert. As a former pastry chef, I truly understand that nothing is more intimidating than baking or making any dessert from scratch, yet at the same time, nothing is quite as satisfying. There is something for everyone in this chapter, from the simplicity of ready-to-eat cookie dough to the sophistication of pots de crème, to the hometown feel of French silk pie. It's bringing a tres leches cake to your nephew's birthday party or rocking the socks off your date with the cold brew rumtini, and it's helping your BFF through her breakup with a pint of the matcha raspberry ice cream. It's another step in knowing that life without dairy is more beautiful than you could have ever imagined.

Orange Cold-Brew Rumtini

makes 2 rumtinis

Is it really the sweetest thing without a cocktail in hand? This is my take on the infamous espresso martini. Instead of a metropolitan vibe, this martini is giving island vibes, which I always prefer. It includes the epically smooth Sweetened Condensed Oat Milk (page 71), proving that you can use that milk for more than just cookies. It's a cocktail that will get you buzzed and keep you dancing all night long.

THE GOODS

4 ounces (120 ml) dark rum
4 ounces (120 ml) cold brew
2 ounces (60 ml) Sweetened Condensed Oat Milk (page 71)
3 dashes of orange bitters
1 ounce (30 ml) aquafaba (liquid from chickpea can)
1¼ cups (150 g) ice
2 orange peel twists

THE METHOD

① Set up your martini glasses so they are ready to be poured. (Extra credit if you first place water with ice cubes in the martini glasses to chill them, then remove the ice water right before pouring the cocktail.)

② Combine all the ingredients, except the ice and orange peels, in a cocktail shaker and "dry shake" vigorously for about 15 seconds. This step will help create a lot of the foam, so put some elbow grease into it. Less shaking = less foam, and more shaking = more foam.

③ Remove the lid and add the ice cubes, then shake again for 30 seconds vigorously. Using a strainer, strain the contents of the shaker into the two chilled martini glasses. Garnish each glass with orange peel twists and enjoy immediately. Cheers to you, boo!

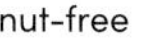
nut-free

gluten-free

soy-free

oil-free

Tiramisu ESPRESSO

serves 2

Imagine the delicate and creamy delight of a tiramisu all wrapped up in your morning espresso. It's the ultimate morning aphrodisiac, best served while still in bed, soaking in every last minute with your new boo—a.k.a. your new dairy-free lifestyle. It's the best of all worlds, dessert, coffee, and something oh-so-indulgent. Want this every day of the week? Prep the Mascarpone Cheese (page 113) ahead of time and your daily coffee-shop stop will be a thing of the past. In this recipe, I used espresso powder so that no matter what your kitchen is stocked with, you can enjoy this in your bathrobe too. Serve over ice, next to fresh flowers, with coffeehouse jazz playing in the distance.

THE GOODS

- ½ cup (120 ml) Mascarpone Cheese (page 113)
- 2 tablespoons (20 g) powdered sugar
- 2 tablespoons (30 ml) unsweetened plant-based milk
- ½ teaspoon pure vanilla extract
- 2 teaspoons instant espresso powder
- ½ cup (60 ml) hot water
- 1 teaspoon unsweetened cacao powder

THE METHOD

First, combine the mascarpone cheese, powdered sugar, plant-based milk, and vanilla in a small bowl, and whisk together for 30 seconds. Set aside in the fridge. Next, combine your instant espresso powder and hot water in a heat-resistant glass and use an electric whisk to blend (alternatively, you can shake well in a mason jar with a lid). Let the espresso mixture cool for 1 to 2 minutes. While it's cooling, prep two rocks glasses by filling them with ice. To serve, pour the espresso mixture over the ice-filled glasses, then divide the creamy mascarpone mixture over the top of both. Garnish each drink with a ½ teaspoon dusting of cacao powder (if you want the superclean look of dusted cacao, use a fine-mesh strainer to sift the cacao over the top). Serve immediately with a spoon; best enjoyed once stirred—and ideally first thing in the morning!

cashew-free

gluten-free

soy-free

grain-free

Oat Chocolate PUT-ON-EVERYTHING SAUCE

makes 16 ounces (2 cups)

For a long time, breaking up with dairy meant breaking up with milk chocolate. Since unsweetened cacao powder is free and clear of dairy, it's really a lifeline for desserts once you finally make the switch. FINALLY, we get to have our milk chocolate. And yes, I put this on *everything*. Okay, almost everything. This is the perfect sauce for ice cream, chocolate milk, hot chocolate, cakes, and . . . your hot date.

THE GOODS

2 cups (480 ml) No-Strain Almond Milk (page 42) or Coconut Milk (page 49)
¾ cup (60 g) unsweetened cacao powder
¼ cup (60 ml) pure maple syrup
2 teaspoons oat flour

THE METHOD

Combine all the ingredients in a medium-size saucepan over medium-low heat, and whisk well. Cook, stirring periodically, for 13 to 15 minutes; if at some point it gets too hot and bubbles over, just lower the heat a bit and whisk to reduce the bubbles. It will reduce a bit and thicken as it cooks. Remove from the heat and let cool completely. Store in an airtight container in the fridge for 7 days. I like to store in a squirt bottle for easy pouring over ice cream and into milk for the perfect chocolate milk! This will thicken a bit once refrigerated but will still pour beautifully once it's chilled.

nut-free optional gluten-free soy-free oil-free

Classic BUTTERCREAM

makes 2 cups

There is nothing quite like the perfect buttercream to make you want to shove your entire face straight into the cake. A buttercream that's just the right amount of sweet and holds up to whatever shape you give it yet melts in your mouth. Go ahead and bookmark this page now because this is the only frosting you'll need, moving forward.

THE GOODS

- 1½ cups (300 g) unsalted vegan butter (see the Butter Block, page 122)
- 1 teaspoon pure vanilla extract
- 2 cups (230 g) organic powdered sugar
- 3 tablespoons (45 ml) plant-based milk

THE METHOD

Remove the butter from the fridge and let sit for 15 to 20 minutes to soften. Combine the softened butter and vanilla in a large stand mixer fitted with a whisk attachment, and mix for 30 seconds. Alternatively, you can use a whisk and get in a great workout by doing this by hand. Add the powdered sugar, 1 cup (115 g) at a time, then slowly pour in the plant-based milk to make it extra fluffy. Whip for a few more seconds, or until you get the perfect consistency. If you live in a cold climate and the butter is taking a while to soften, or is not softening on the countertop, pop the butter into your stand mixer and add the plant milk first. You get a better result when you add the milk last, but it's an easy work-around for those in cold climates. Store in the fridge quickly as it will melt if left out for too long. Will keep for 7 days.

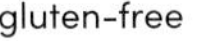

soy-free

grain-free

WHIPPED CREAM
Two Ways

makes 15 to 18 ounces

Have you ever orgasmed the second you put something in your mouth? If not, this is the recipe for you. Not only is it rich and fulfilling, it doesn't play favorites: regardless of what you have on hand, or what your food allergies are, there's a version for you. The key is to chill either the canned coconut cream or the silken tofu overnight so you get the perfect consistency.

THE GOODS

Soy:

16 ounces (450 g) cold silken tofu, drained and patted dry
¼ cup (40 g) powdered sugar
½ teaspoon pure vanilla extract
1 teaspoon freshly squeezed lemon juice

Coconut:

1 (13½-ounce [398 ml]) can coconut cream, chilled
1 tablespoon (15 ml) pure maple syrup
½ teaspoon pure vanilla extract

THE METHOD

Soy version: Combine the tofu, powdered sugar, vanilla, and lemon juice in a stand mixer fitted with the whisk attachment. Whisk on high speed for 4 to 5 minutes, or until everything is combined and very soft peaks start to form. Best enjoyed fresh, but otherwise pour it into a Glasslock container, refrigerate, and consume within 2 to 3 days.

Coconut version: Scoop the coconut fat off the top of the coconut cream and only use this for the recipe; save the coconut water at the bottom for something else. Combine the coconut fat, maple syrup, and vanilla in a stand mixer fitted with the whisk attachment. Whisk on high speed for 4 to 5 minutes, or until everything is combined and very soft peaks start to form. Best enjoyed fresh, but otherwise pour it into a Glasslock container, refrigerate, and consume within 2 to 3 days.

nut-free optional

gluten-free

soy-free optional

grain-free

oil-free

Double CHOCOLATE CHAI-SPICED HAZELNUT SPREAD + Coffee Creamer

makes 14 to 16 ounces (1¾ to 2 cups)

Here's everyone's favorite spread turned up a notch and even transformed into your new favorite coffee creamer. Making your own dairy-free Nutella at home takes a bit of patience, and this process absolutely requires a food processor. What I'm saying is, don't try to make this in your blender as it will leave you frustrated and very unsatisfied. This spread has the perfect amount of chai-inspired spices, paired with cacao and melted dark chocolate. Regardless of whether you eat this with berries or on toast, or turn it into a dirty chai latte, you'll never go back to the store-bought spread again.

THE GOODS

- 3 cups (420 g) roasted unsalted hazelnuts
- 5 tablespoons (20 g) unsweetened cacao powder
- ¼ cup (60 ml) pure maple syrup
- 1 teaspoon pure vanilla extract
- ½ teaspoon ground cinnamon
- ¼ teaspoon ground ginger
- ¼ teaspoon ground cloves
- ¼ teaspoon ground cardamom
- Pinch of salt
- 1¾ cups (420 ml) unsweetened No-Strain Almond Milk (page 42)
- 1 cup (240 ml) melted dairy-free dark chocolate

THE METHOD

① Roast the hazelnuts for 10 minutes at 200°F (93°C). Remove from the oven and place on one side of a clean dish towel, then fold and cover with the other side, with the nuts inside. Gently press down and move your hands back

recipe continues →

cashew-free

gluten-free

soy-free

grain-free

oil-free

and forth to try to remove most of the hazelnut skins. Transfer the hazelnuts to a food processor. Process on low speed for 10 to 15 minutes, or until they become a smooth paste. Patience is the key here, and you may need to scrape down the sides every few minutes with a spatula.

② When you have a paste, add the rest of the ingredients, one at a time, still on low speed, and process for another few minutes. When you add the melted chocolate last, blend for 30 more seconds after you have a smooth mixture. Place in an airtight container and refrigerate for 10 to 14 days.

Coffee creamer: In a blender, combine ¼ cup (60 ml) of the finished spread with 1 cup (240 ml) of water and blend on high speed until smooth. Add to your coffee and swoon a little bit. Store the rest in a mason jar in the fridge for up to a week.

cashew-free gluten-free soy-free grain-free oil-free

Granola Cookie Dough MILKSHAKE

makes two 14- to 16-ounce milkshakes

There's no milk or ice cream in this shake! Not only is this a recipe for the most delicious milkshake, but you also get a bonus high-protein and allergy-friendly cookie dough recipe too. Ahead of assembly, you'll need to make the two batches of Granola Milk (page 53), freeze 2½ cups (290 g) of it into ice cubes, and chill the rest, then make and freeze the cookie dough (spoiler alert: garbanzos are the secret ingredient). Add it all together with the reserved granola milk and you have yourself the most epic vegan cinnamon cookie dough milkshake without any fillers, gums, refined sugar, or BS. Keep the ice cubes and cookie dough ready to go in your freezer so you have it whenever life calls for a milkshake fix.

THE GOODS

Edible Cookie Dough:

1 (15-ounce can [425 g]) garbanzo beans (chickpeas), drained and rinsed
½ teaspoon pure vanilla extract
½ cup (130 g) sunflower butter (almond butter works too!)
½ cup (240 ml) pure maple syrup
¼ teaspoon salt
1 cup (110 g) oat flour
½ cup (90 g) dairy-free chocolate chips

Milkshake:

2½ cups (290 g) Granola Milk (page 53) ice cubes
2 cups (480 ml) Granola Milk (page 53)
1 cup (120 g) frozen cookie dough, rough chopped, plus more for garnish

THE METHOD

① ***First, make your cookie dough:*** Combine all the dough ingredients, except the chocolate chips, in a food processor. Blend on high speed for 2 to 3 minutes, or until fully mixed. Then, add the chocolate chips and blend again for 5 to 10 seconds, to mix in the chips without crumbling them up. Line a large baking sheet with parchment paper. Press the dough onto the parchment into a large rectangle about ½ inch

recipe continues →

gluten-free

thick. Freeze the dough for 4 or more hours. Once the dough is frozen, remove from the freezer and cut into small bite-size pieces on a cutting board. Act quickly because the dough softens rapidly. Once all the dough is cut into bite-size pieces, transfer them to an airtight container and freeze until it's time to make your milkshakes.

② ***Make the shakes:*** Combine the granola milk ice cubes and granola milk in a high-powered blender and blend on high speed for 15 seconds. You may have to use an accelerator stick to help get everything moving. Toss 1 cup (120 g) of the frozen cookie dough pieces into the blender. Blend on high speed for 15 to 20 seconds. Serve immediately while still cold, garnished with extra cookie dough bites.

gluten-free

Spiced POTS DE CRÈME

makes two 8-ounce pots

Pots de crème got together with Mexican hot chocolate and made this epic combination. This recipe uses easy-to-find pantry ingredients and can easily be made completely allergy-friendly. This is so much more than just "a jar of cream"; it's luxurious, it's spicy, and it's the best dessert to bring over to your friend's house for wine night, or the perfect addition to a bougie park picnic.

THE GOODS

1 tablespoon (8 g) tapioca starch or cornstarch
1 tablespoon (15 ml) water
2 cups (480 ml) No-Strain Almond Milk (page 42) or Oat Hemp Milk (page 45)
½ cup (80 g) coconut sugar
⅓ cup (25 g) unsweetened cacao powder
½ teaspoon ground cinnamon, plus more for garnish
¼ teaspoon cayenne pepper, plus more for garnish
Pinch of salt
½ cup (90 g) vegan chocolate chips
1 teaspoon pure vanilla extract
Coconut Whipped Cream (page 262)

THE METHOD

① Set a few 8-ounce (240 ml) mason jars or containers near your stovetop, for the finished custards.

② Stir the tapioca starch with the water in a small bowl until it's all dissolved, then set aside.

③ Combine the almond milk, coconut sugar, cacao powder, cinnamon, cayenne, and salt in a 3-quart saucepan over medium heat, and begin to whisk. Cook, whisking every few seconds, for 10 minutes. Don't walk away from this one; the mixture will begin to bubble and thicken, and can bubble over very quickly if you have your back turned. After 10 minutes, add the chocolate chips and vanilla, and keep whisking until the chocolate is melted, in 1 to 2 minutes. Pour in the tapioca mixture next, and cook over medium heat, whisking constantly, for 1 to 2 minutes. The mixture will begin to thicken quickly. Remove from the heat and quickly pour the mixture into your jars. Let cool for 5 minutes, then cap with a lid and let the pots de crème set in the fridge for at least 4 hours. Best chilled overnight. Serve with the whipped cream and a sprinkle of cayenne or cinnamon.

nut-free optional

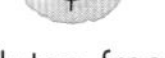
gluten-free

soy-free

grain-free optional

oil-free

Black Sesame BLACKBERRY FLAN

serves 2 to 4

setting time: 6 hours

When you see the Black Sesame Seed Milk (page 57), you might be thinking, *Where the hell am I going to use this?* and obviously, the answer is right here on this page. Flan is so custardy and truly unique in the world of sweets. There are so many kinds of custards across so many different cultures, but what makes flan so special is the layer of wet caramel that glistens and falls over the top. No egg yolks and heavy cream are needed here, as we use agar-agar to hold the custard together, paired with the black sesame seed milk and blackberries to make a truly one-of-a-kind flan.

THE GOODS

Blackberry Caramel:

¼ cup (40 g) coconut sugar
¼ cup (60 ml) water
8–10 (70 g) blackberries, plus more for garnish

Black Sesame Seed Milk Flan:

1¼ cups (300 ml) Black Sesame Seed Milk (page 57)
1 (13½-ounce [398 ml]) can coconut cream
⅓ cup (55 g) coconut sugar
1 tablespoon (7g) tapioca starch
1 teaspoon agar-agar

THE METHOD

① Have a 9-inch cake or springform pan, or three 3-inch-diameter flat-bottomed containers on standby here.

② *Make the blackberry caramel:* Combine the coconut sugar, water, and blackberries in a high-powered blender and blend on high speed for 15 seconds, or until you have a puree. Pour the mixture into a small saucepan and cook over medium-low heat for 7 to 8 minutes, or until you have a thick blackberry sauce. Set aside.

③ *Make the flan:* Combine the black sesame seed milk, coconut cream, coconut sugar, tapioca starch, and agar-agar in a high-powered blender and blend on high speed for 60 seconds. Pour

recipe continues →

cashew-free

gluten-free

soy-free

grain-free

oil-free

the liquid into a small, heavy-bottomed saucepan and cook over medium heat, stirring constantly with a rubber spatula, for 9 to 10 minutes. If it bubbles over too much, lower the heat and keep cooking and stirring. Once the mixture has become a thicker consistency but is still semi-runny and coats the back of a spoon, remove from the heat and set aside.

④ Pour the blackberry caramel sauce into your pan or three smaller containers, then carefully pour the hot flan mixture from the blender over the top. Let cool for 20 minutes. Cover and place in the fridge for 6 or more hours or overnight, to set.

⑤ To serve, using a butter knife, carefully cut around the edges of the pan or containers. Then, place a serving plate (or an individual serving plate if you used a small container) upside down on top of the flan. Pick up both the flan pan/container and the plate, and flip over quickly. Now, the flan, will be upside down on the plate. Carefully remove the flan pan/container by lifting upward, and voilà, you have a flan with the blackberry sauce on the top, running down the sides!

⑥ Enjoy cold with extra blackberries.

cashew-free

gluten-free

soy-free

grain-free

oil-free

Almond French SILK PIE

makes one 10-inch pie

This pie needs no introduction. It's a classic that, honestly, if I left you all alone with, I wouldn't doubt you'd eat the entire thing by yourself. It's the ultimate cure for any bad day, or the perfect dessert to bring to a dinner party. The crust itself is gluten-free and can be used for any sweet pie, so feel free to mix and match it with another pie recipe you love! The chocolate filling could also be made into a high-protein pudding, so if you don't feel like making a whole pie and want to snack on some pudding, live your best life and go for it.

THE GOODS

Piecrust:

½ cup (55 g) oat flour, plus more for dusting
1½ cups (165 g) almond flour
1 teaspoon salt
2 tablespoons (20 g) coconut sugar (sub cane sugar for coconut allergy)
5 tablespoons (75 g) cold salted butter (see Salted Butter Block, page 122)
¼ cup (60 ml) ice-cold water

Chocolate Filling:

1 (14-ounce [400 g]) block firm tofu, drained
1 large avocado, pitted and peeled
¼ cup (60 ml) almond butter
¾ cup (120 g) coconut sugar (sub cane sugar for coconut allergy)
1 teaspoon pure vanilla extract
¼ cup (20 g) unsweetened cacao powder
½ cup (120 ml) No-Strain Almond Milk (page 42)
¼ cup (60 ml) pure maple syrup
1 cup (150 g) melted vegan chocolate chips

Garnishes:

1 batch Whipped Cream (page 262)
1 (3.5-ounce [100 g]) vegan chocolate bar, sliced into small shavings or slivers

THE METHOD

① You'll need a 10-inch pie pan, so set that aside.

② *Make the piecrust:* Combine the oat flour, almond flour, salt, and coconut sugar in a bowl, and mix well with a fork. Add the cold butter and incorporate with the fork or your fingers until you get little pea-size balls of butter within the flour blend. Then, add the ice-cold water, 1 tablespoon at a time, until you are able to form a dough. Depending on where you live and the humidity, you might need a little more, or a little less water. Press the mixture into a large dough ball and be careful

recipe continues →

gluten-free

not to overmix. Wrap the dough in parchment paper and let chill in the fridge for 15 minutes. You can do this step up to a day ahead of time.

③ Preheat the oven to 350°F (177°C). Unwrap the dough, keeping it on the parchment, on a large cutting board. Sprinkle a bit more oat flour (about 1 tablespoon [7 g]) on top of the dough ball, then top with another large piece of parchment. Using a rolling pin, roll out the dough between the parchment papers until you get a size that fits the edges of the pie pan. Remove the top layer of the parchment carefully at an angle so you don't disrupt the crust. Then, place the pie pan, face down, on the crust. Grab the bottom of the cutting board with one hand, and the pie pan with the other, and flip them (this is easier with two people). Then, remove the parchment and let the crust relax into the pan. It will not be perfect, but use this as a base and begin to press any dough from the top edges of the pie pan into the center and the sides if there are cracks or holes. Once the inside is covered evenly with crust, take a fork and pierce the crust two or three times. Bake for 25 minutes, remove from the oven, and let cool completely.

④ ***Make the chocolate filling***: Combine all its ingredients, except the melted chocolate, in a high-powered blender or a food processor, and blend on medium-low speed until smooth. You will need to use the accelerator for this one if using the blender; so if you don't have that option, stick to using a food processor. Once the mixture is smooth, quickly pour the melted chocolate into the blender and blend on high speed for 30 more seconds. Pour the mixture into the fully cooled piecrust, cover, then let it chill in the fridge for 4 hours.

⑤ After about 4 hours, or when ready to serve, spread the entire batch of whipped cream on top of the pie, then garnish with the chocolate shavings. Enjoy immediately, or keep in the fridge, covered, until ready to serve. Best enjoyed within 5 to 7 days.

gluten-free

Mandarin Mango POSSET

makes 20 possets; serves 8

We couldn't hit all the recipes for a creamy custard without making a posset. Posset is an epically easy dessert to make and is just another reminder of how delicious and fun a dairy-free life can be. Of course, I had to add my beachside twist by making this one out of mandarins and garnishing with a Tajín twist. It's the best dessert for a summer barbecue, and if you're really wanting to turn it up, these little guys pair perfectly with a shot of mezcal. If it's an extra-hot summer, freeze these for a few minutes to turn this posset into a thirst-quenching sorbet.

THE GOODS

10 mandarins
1 small yellow mango, or 1 cup (130 g) frozen mango
⅓ cup (60 g) organic cane sugar
1 (13.5-ounce [398 g]) can coconut cream, chilled overnight
Tajín or chili salt, or thinly sliced lime wedges, for garnish

THE METHOD

① Cut the mandarin oranges in half and then use a spoon to scoop out the center of each orange. Be careful to leave all the peel intact, as you will use all ten of them to contain the custard. While scooping out the peels, place the fruit from four of the mandarins in a high-powered blender. Save the rest of the fruit from the other six mandarins for a smoothie later on, discarding any parts that are very white and pithy. Add the mango and cane sugar to the blender. Finally, scoop the fat off the top of the coconut cream and add to the blender. Save the clear coconut water for a smoothie later on! Blend for about 2 minutes, or until everything is smooth.

② Pour the mixture into a saucepan and cook over medium-low heat, stirring every few minutes, for 10 minutes or so, until it is thick enough to coat the back of a spoon. Pour the custard from the pan into the orange shells and arrange them on a dish, so they can set in the refrigerator, then cover with plastic wrap. Refrigerate for 6 hours to overnight. Serve with Tajín or thinly sliced lime wedges.

③ To make sorbet, transfer the custard-filled mandarins to a freezer-safe container and freeze for an hour. These will keep for 5 days in an airtight container in the fridge or 10 days in the freezer.

cashew-free

gluten-free

soy-free

oil-free

Raspberry Matcha NO-CHURN ICE CREAM

makes 2 pints

It's no secret that I am purely addicted to matcha. It's loaded with antioxidants and has L-theanine, an amino acid that helps you avoid the post-caffeine crash, a.k.a. the perfect way to get that morning buzz. This no-churn ice cream is as easy to make as it sounds and is the perfect remedy to the dating blues. This will help soothe the soul while also helping you get hyped up to get back out there. It's a reminder that you can sit on the couch and eat a pint of ice cream and still be an empowered independent woman (or man) who doesn't let the end of a relationship get her down for too long.

setting time: 6 hours

THE GOODS

2 (13.5-ounce [398 ml]) cans coconut cream fat, chilled
1 teaspoon matcha powder
¼ cup + 1 tablespoon (75 ml) pure maple syrup
½ teaspoon pure vanilla extract

Raspberry Jam:
1 heaping cup (150 g) fresh or frozen raspberries
¼ cup (60 ml) water
¼ cup (60 ml) pure maple syrup
1 tablespoon (3 g) lemon zest

THE METHOD

① Scoop the fat off the top of the cold coconut cream and place in a large stand mixer or a bowl with a handheld electric mixer. Save the clear coconut water for another use. Mix on high speed for 60 seconds until whipped. Toss in the matcha, maple syrup, and vanilla, and mix again for 30 seconds. Then, pour into a freezer-safe container. Cap with a lid and place in the freezer for 2 hours—not any longer because you will have trouble folding in the raspberry jam later.

② *Prepare the jam:* Combine all the jam ingredients in a saucepan, and cook over medium-low heat for 10 minutes, or until most of the liquid has reduced. Remove from the heat and let cool completely. I like to just let this sit out while the ice cream freezes for the first round. After 2 hours, remove the ice cream from the freezer; it should be semisoft. Fold in the raspberry jam to make raspberry swirls. Put a lid back on and let freeze for at least 4 more hours. Enjoy with your favorite rom-com!

tip * **Add a shot of vodka to the initial mixture to keep it creamy for days.**

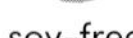

cashew-free gluten-free soy-free grain-free oil-free

Peanut Butter Caramel SWIRL BLONDIES

makes one 9-inch square pan

Caramel swirl blondies = two recipes in one. First up, we've got, by far, some of the best homemade caramel ever. All you need are two ingredients and thirty minutes, and you'll end up with a caramel that goes so well in coffee, on apples, and pretty much in just about anything you want to take to the next level—you'll have extra caramel to try them all! It could even work as a sweet treat for your next date, if you know what I'm saying. Second, this recipe for blondies uses whole plant-based ingredients, making them gluten-free, high in protein, oil-free, and low in sugar. It's everything you could want in a dessert, and I promise that the kiddos won't even know that it's good for them too.

THE GOODS

Caramel:

1 cup (160 g) coconut sugar
1 cup (240 ml) Coconut Milk (page 49), or full-fat canned

Blondies:

1 (16-ounce [454 g]) can garbanzo beans (chickpeas), drained
1 cup (240 ml) applesauce
¼ cup (60 ml) Coconut Milk (page 49), or full-fat canned
½ cup (120 ml) peanut butter
½ cup (80 g) coconut sugar
½ teaspoon pure vanilla extract
1 cup (100 g) oat flour
½ teaspoon salt
½ teaspoon baking soda
½ teaspoon baking powder
1 teaspoon coconut oil (optional)

THE METHOD

① *Make the caramel:* Whisk together the coconut sugar and coconut milk in a small saucepan over medium-high heat and keep whisking. Once the mixture starts to bubble over, lower the heat to medium-low and cook, stirring occasionally, for 25 to 30 minutes. Once the liquid has reduced by half and becomes much thicker, remove from the heat and let cool completely. If

recipe continues →

cashew-free

gluten-free

soy-free

oil-free optional

you want the caramel to be a bit thicker, let chill in the fridge for a few hours, and that will do the trick.

② *Make the blondies:* Preheat the oven to 350°F (177°C). Combine the garbanzo beans, applesauce, coconut milk, peanut butter, coconut sugar, and vanilla in a food processor, and process on high speed for about 2 minutes, or until everything is combined/smooth. Combine the oat flour, salt, baking soda, and baking powder in a small bowl, and mix well. Slowly add the flour mixture to the food processor and process on high speed for about 60 more seconds, or until the mixture is smooth.

③ Line a 9-inch square pan with parchment paper or oil it with coconut oil, then pour the blondie batter into the prepared pan. Spoon out about half the caramel into dollops on the top of the blondie batter and use a toothpick or chopstick to gently swirl the caramel into the batter. Bake for 55 to 60 minutes. Remove from the oven and let cool for about 30 minutes before enjoying. Store, covered and airtight, in the fridge for up to 5 days.

cashew-free

gluten-free

soy-free

oil-free optional

Blueberry Mermaid CUPCAKES

makes 12 or 13 cupcakes

These cupcakes are not only a celebration of your post-dairy glow-up, but they are as beautiful as you have become during this process. It's a glow that stems from eating compassionately, clearing up your skin, becoming a home chef, and focusing on yourself, and your inner wealth. Butterfly pea powder gives the frosting the mermaid turquoise color and is also a natural and incredible source of antioxidants. You can easily find it online or in the superfood section of your grocery store. If you can't find it, use matcha powder instead. I prefer to use frozen wild blueberries for the cupcakes because they have the most antioxidants and make the cupcakes the most beautiful blue color.

THE GOODS

1½ cups (360 ml) unsweetened plant-based milk, at room temperature
1 tablespoon (15 ml) cider vinegar
1 teaspoon pure vanilla extract
⅓ cup (80 ml) melted coconut oil
2½ cups (375 g) 1-to-1 gluten-free flour, or spelt or all-purpose flour
½ teaspoon baking soda
1 tablespoon (15 g) baking powder
Pinch of salt
1 cup (160 g) coconut sugar, plus more for sprinkling
1 cup (140 g) frozen or fresh blueberries
1 batch Classic Buttercream (page 261)
1 teaspoon butterfly pea powder
Edible glitter (optional)

THE METHOD

① Preheat the oven to 350°F (177°C). Line a cupcake pan with parchment liners or silicone molds and set aside.

② Combine the plant-based milk, cider vinegar, and vanilla in a small bowl, and stir with a spoon until mixed. Pour in the melted coconut oil and mix. Set aside.

③ Combine the flour, baking soda, baking powder, salt, and coconut sugar in a large bowl,

recipe continues →

gluten-free optional

soy-free

and mix with a fork. Now, slowly stir the wet ingredients into the dry ingredients. Mix with a spatula just until you have a smooth batter; be careful to not overmix it. Once the batter is combined, fold in the blueberries.

④ Fill up each prepared cupcake well three-quarters full, leaving room for them to expand while cooking. Sprinkle some coconut sugar over the top. Bake for 25 to 28 minutes, or until a toothpick comes out clean from the center. Remove from the oven and let cool completely before adding the buttercream frosting.

⑤ To make the mermaid buttercream frosting, follow the instructions for Classic Buttercream (page 261) adding the butterfly pea powder when you add the powdered sugar. Transfer the icing to a piping bag and pipe the frosting over the cupcakes, or go the old-fashioned route and use a knife to swirl with the buttercream. Sprinkle with edible glitter (if using) and serve! Will keep in an airtight container in the fridge for 3 to 4 days.

gluten-free optional

soy-free

Mini Churro CORN CAKES with Macerated PEACHES

serves 20

I first made these corn cakes for a pop-up dinner benefit for one of my favorite animal sanctuaries here in So-Cal, Sale Ranch. They're moist, perfectly sweet, and coated with plant butter, cinnamon, and coconut sugar. As I put out the large baking sheets to serve seventy people, I realized this recipe was meant to be shared with community. After all, that's how we can work together to create real and lasting change. Here, this recipe serves twenty and can be made either on a large baking sheet or in mini Bundt cake pans. Halve it for a smaller party; multiply by three and you'll feed your neighborhood. Since we're on a mission to get us all to break up with dairy, this is an epic place to start and spread the love.

THE GOODS

- 1½ cups (360 ml) melted salted vegan butter (see the Butter Block, page 122), plus more for brushing pan
- 3 tablespoons (20 g) ground chia seeds or flaxseed meal
- ⅓ cup (80 ml) water
- ¾ cup (180 ml) applesauce
- 3 cups (720 ml) No-Strain Almond Milk (page 42)
- 2 tablespoons (30 ml) cider vinegar
- 1 cup (240 ml) pure maple syrup
- 1½ cups (240 g) coconut sugar (sub cane sugar for coconut allergy)
- 3 cups (420 g) cornmeal
- 3 cups (450 g) 1-to-1 gluten-free baking flour
- 1 tablespoon (12 g) baking soda
- 2 tablespoons (25 g) baking powder
- ¾ teaspoon salt
- 3 tablespoons (20 g) ground cinnamon
- Oat Chocolate Put-on-Everything Sauce (page 258)

Peaches:

- 6 peaches, pitted and sliced
- ¼ cup (60 ml) fresh orange juice
- ¼ cup (40 g) coconut sugar (sub cane sugar for coconut allergy)
- 1 tablespoon (7 g) ground cinnamon

gluten-free

soy-free

THE METHOD

① Preheat your oven to 350°F (177°C). Prep either a large baking sheet or a mini Bundt pan by brushing melted butter over the bottom; set aside.

② Make a "chia egg" by combining the ground chia seeds and water in a large bowl and stirring for 60 seconds until you have a jellylike consistency. Now, add the applesauce, almond milk, cider vinegar, maple syrup, 1 cup (160 g) of the coconut sugar, and 1 cup (240 ml) of the melted butter, and whisk for 1 to 2 minutes, or until everything is fully incorporated. Set aside.

③ Combine the cornmeal, gluten-free flour blend, baking soda, baking powder, and salt in a small bowl, and stir with a fork until everything is fully mixed. Now, slowly add the cornmeal mixture to the almond milk mixture, stirring constantly, until you have a thick batter. Once your batter is fully mixed, set it aside for 5 to 10 minutes to set.

④ Then, either pour it onto the prepared baking sheet or into the prepared mini Bundt pan wells, filling them three-quarters full to leave room for expansion. Bake for 25 minutes, or until the top is firm and golden brown. Remove from the oven and let cool.

⑤ ***Make the macerated peaches:*** Combine the sliced peaches, orange juice, coconut sugar, and cinnamon in a bowl and mix until the peaches are fully coated. Set aside.

⑥ Sprinkle the remaining ½ cup (80 g) of coconut sugar and 3 tablespoons (20 g) of cinnamon on a plate or in a small bowl, and mix well. Flip over the cooled baking sheet cake or remove the mini Bundt cakes and flip them over so they are on their flat side. Using a pastry brush, brush your last ½ cup (120 ml) of melted butter over the top of the baking sheet cake or each mini cake. Dust with the cinnamon sugar or gently roll each cake in it.

⑦ Serve warm with the macerated fruit and drizzle with the chocolate sauce. Store the cakes, the fruit, and the chocolate sauce separately. The cake and chocolate sauce will keep about 5 days in the fridge; the fruit, only about 24 hours.

gluten-free

soy-free

Chocolate Chunk FUDGE POPS

makes 12 pops

This recipe here is for the kids—okay, and for the adults too. With schools requiring allergy-friendly treats, and since parents have the most stressful job of all, I wanted to take off some of the stress of this breakup and give you a recipe that is a 10/10 every single time. It's refined sugar-free, and made with only a few ingredients—easy-peasy prep. You can even wrap the pops individually in parchment paper to make the grab-and-go that much easier!

THE GOODS

1 batch Oat Hemp Milk (page 45)
½ cup (35 g) unsweetened cacao powder
½ cup (120 ml) pure maple syrup
1 tablespoon (7 g) tapioca starch
2 tablespoons (30 ml) water
1 cup (160 g) vegan chocolate chips, chopped

THE METHOD

Combine the milk, cacao powder, and maple syrup in a medium-size saucepan. Whisk well, then cook on medium-low heat for 10 minutes. Meanwhile, combine the tapioca starch and water in a small bowl. Next, add the tapioca mixture and the chocolate chips to the milk mixture and whisk while cooking for another 3 minutes. Remove from the heat, transfer to a large bowl, and let cool for about 10 minutes. When the chocolate mixture has cooled enough to not be hot to the touch, pour into ice pop molds and freeze for 6 hours. Best consumed within a month.

nut-free

gluten-free

soy-free

oil-free

S'more MUG CAKE

makes 2 mug cakes

Sometimes, all you want is a single serving of a freshly made cake without having to drive to a bakery or feel that it is a "guilty pleasure." In this post-breakup world, there is no such thing as a guilty pleasure; it's all the pleasure with none of the guilt. This mug cake is made in less than five minutes with ingredients you can find in your pantry. And I'm just going to say, you can have it any time of the day: with your coffee for breakfast, with your afternoon meeting, or even as the best midnight snack.

THE GOODS

3 tablespoons (20 g) almond flour
3 tablespoons (25 g) oat flour
3 tablespoons (15 g) unsweetened cacao powder
3 tablespoons (30 g) coconut sugar (sub organic cane sugar for coconut allergy)
¼ teaspoon baking soda
½ cup (120 ml) No-Strain Almond Milk (page 42)
¼ cup (60 ml) almond butter
½ teaspoon pure vanilla extract
¾ cup (115 g) vegan chocolate chips
¾ cup (65 g) mini vegan marshmallows
¼ teaspoon flaky sea salt

THE METHOD

Combine the almond flour, oat flour, cacao, coconut sugar, and baking soda in a medium-size bowl and mix well with a fork. Then, add the almond milk, almond butter, and vanilla. Mix until the consistency is supersmooth. Fold in the chocolate chips and marshmallows. Pour into two 12-ounce microwave-safe mugs, filling each halfway full. Microwave in 30-second increments until the cake is to your liking: cook for three 30-second rounds for a brownie-like cake, or go four or five 30-second rounds for a fluffier cake. Enjoy immediately with a cup of coffee or scoop of vegan ice cream!

gluten-free

soy-free

oil-free

Pistachio CRÈME BRÛLÉE

makes 4 crème brûlées

Oh, what I would give to serve this crème brûlée to some of my old French chef instructors and mentors. After all, in the eyes of French food, a dairy-free crème brûlée is pretty sinful. Luckily, we're here to challenge the norms and change the status quo, so this recipe fits the bill. I absolutely love using the pistachio milk for this recipe for that extra layer of decadence. You'll need to plan ahead, since it needs an overnight sit. It's a classic crème brûlée with a modern twist, best served up with a piping-hot cup of saving the world through food.

THE GOODS

3 cups (720 ml) Pistachio Milk (page 54)
¼ cup (60 ml) agave nectar
⅓ cup (50 g) tapioca starch
¼ teaspoon spirulina
Pinch of salt
½ cup (110 g) white organic cane sugar

THE METHOD

① Simply combine all the ingredients, except the white cane sugar, in a high-powered blender and blend until smooth, for 10 to 15 seconds. Pour into a saucepan and whisk over medium to medium-low heat for 7 minutes, or until it becomes thick and custard-like. Then, remove from the heat and let cool for 5 to 10 minutes. Pour the mixture into smaller serving dishes; I like to use a couple of crème brûlée ramekins for a little added aesthetic. Cover with plastic wrap, letting the plastic touch the custard so it doesn't create condensation, and then set in the fridge overnight.

② The next day, transfer the brûlées from the fridge and carefully remove the plastic wrap. Working one at a time, coat the top with a generous amount of cane sugar and then use a pastry torch to caramelize the sugar. If you don't have a pastry torch, you can put these under the broiler on HIGH for 2 to 4 minutes. Keep an eye on them, as the time will vary, depending on how hot your broiler gets. Serve immediately!

cashew-free

gluten-free

soy-free

grain-free

Vanilla Nut-Nog
TRES LECHES CAKE

makes one 9-inch round cake

A true test of your dairy-free skills is to bring a family favorite, like a tres leches cake, for the holidays and tell no one it's dairy-free, vegan, and (if you use GF flour) gluten-free, and see what happens. Not only do I promise everyone will love this rendition, but it will quickly become the yearly must-bring dish. She's festive, so damn flavorful, and truly a dairy-free dream.

THE GOODS

1 teaspoon coconut oil, for pan
2¾ cups (660 ml) Vanilla Nut-Nog (page 58)
1½ cups (360 ml) Coconut Milk (page 49), at room temperature
1 teaspoon cider vinegar
½ cup (120 ml) melted coconut oil
1½ cups (225 g) 1-to-1 gluten-free baking flour or all-purpose flour
½ cup (60 g) coconut flour
2 teaspoons baking powder
½ teaspoon baking soda
¾ cup (120 g) coconut sugar
¼ teaspoon salt
1 batch Coconut Whipped Cream (page 262)
½ teaspoon ground cinnamon
Pomegranate seeds

THE METHOD

① Preheat the oven to 350°F (177°C). Oil a 9-inch round cake pan with the teaspoon of coconut oil. Set aside. Combine 1¾ cups (420 ml) of the nut-nog, 1 cup (240 ml) of the coconut milk, the cider vinegar, and the melted coconut oil in a large bowl. Set aside.

② Combine the GF flour, coconut flour, baking powder, baking soda, coconut sugar, and salt in another bowl with a spatula or a stand mixer fitted with the paddle attachment. Mix well and then slowly add the nut-nog mixture to the flour mixture. When the batter is fully mixed, stop—be careful not to overmix! Pour the batter into the prepared cake pan. Bake for 20 to 25 minutes, or until a toothpick stuck into the center of the cake comes out clean. Remove from the oven and let the cake cool completely.

③ Mix the remaining ½ cup (120 ml) of coconut milk with the remaining cup (240 ml) of nut-nog. (You'll have extra nut-nog.) Once the cake is cool, use a fork to poke about ten holes in the center and then gently pour the nut-nog mixture over the top of the cake. Let the nut-nog mixture set into the cake for about 30 minutes in the fridge before you top with an entire batch of whipped cream, a sprinkle of cinnamon, and a generous amount of pomegranate seeds. Serve cold. Best consumed within 5 to 7 days.

cashew-free

gluten-free optional

soy-free

Acknowledgments

I have so many people to thank for this book, but the most important person to thank is my husband, Steve. This is a work of his dedication, his photography, and his true patience with me and the art of vegan cheesemaking. We spent an entire year together putting everything to the side and investing all our resources so that we could get every single recipe *just right*. He is as much a part of this as I am and truly deserves an award for the amount of dishes, emotional fires, and sweaty days in the kitchen we went through together. Everyone needs a Steve in their life, and I'm just happy I get to work with and cowrite with mine.

Along with my husband, I, of course, want to shout out my family for willing to take this ride with us and break up with dairy too. We have been fighting heart disease for generations, and for the first time, I feel like we can be the change within our lineage. My mom got her coffee creamer and my dad got his chiles relleno while we change the course of our future and our health. It takes a lot to go against culture, against what we're taught, and to admit that things need to change. So thank you for being willing to take off the rose-colored glasses and step into truth with me. As I always say, breakups are better done together.

To my friend Carleigh, from the minute I shared this book concept with you, you have been one of my biggest supporters and cheerleaders. It's not often that you can connect with someone and build a friendship online all while living in different countries, but thank god we did! Thank you for being a sounding board, for writing the best foreword, and for connecting me with Wendy. Your support changed the course of this book!

Wendy, you are the literary agent of my dreams. Thank you for always being in my corner and for believing in me and this book from the moment you read the proposal. Being an author is so much easier with an agent like you in my corner!

To everyone at Balance, especially my editor Renee. It's rare you find an editor who really sees you and can see the world from a similar perspective. Writing and editing with you has been so easy, and I really looked forward to every single step of this book-writing process because I knew you would just *get it.* And thanks to Cisca Schreefel, Nyamekye Waliyaya, Toni Tajima, Amanda Kain, Nzinga Temu, Kara Brammer, and Kindall Gant. Looking forward to writing many more books together with the entire team.

I also want to show my sincere gratitude to one of my best friends, George, who hand made a lot of the plates and bowls shown throughout the photography. George, you are forever one of my favorite people and to know a piece of you is in this book makes it that much more meaningful.

To Jen and the entire team from Sale Ranch. I have been inspired by your compassion and dedication to not only your animals at the sanctuary but to all animals and what they go through. Not many people can do what you do and really face the harsh realities of animal agriculture and be able to rehab animals that by some miracle made it out alive. I am so grateful our paths crossed and we can continue to fight for a better world together. Thanks for letting me come to the ranch and love on the cows and goats so they could get their moment to shine.

And finally, the best for last. Thank you to this entire community. From my first *Breaking Up with Dairy* TikTok, you all have been the fuel that kept the fire burning, you all made me realize that I wasn't alone in how truly hard this breakup could be, and your unwavering support literally made my dreams come true. Together we can make real change for ourselves, the planet, and for the cows and goats and sheep that need us to fight for them. I know this is only the beginning!

All my love,

Bai

References

World Number of Lactose Intolerance:
https://www.niddk.nih.gov/health-information/digestive-diseases/lactose-intolerance

Calcium, Dairy, and "Strong Bones":
https://www.ncbi.nlm.nih.gov/pmc/articles/PMC4784799/

Phytoestrogens (Soy Products) and Their Health Benefits:
https://www.ncbi.nlm.nih.gov/pmc/articles/PMC6390141/

World Use of Soy Products:
https://ourworldindata.org/soy

Dairy Consumption and Breast Cancer:
https://www.pcrm.org/news/blog/us-meat-and-dairy-companies-spend-millions-lobbying-against-climate-legislation

Dairy and Cancer:
Kakkoura, M. G., H. Du, Y. Guo, et al. "Dairy Consumption and Risks of Total and Site-Specific Cancers in Chinese Adults: An 11-Year Prospective Study of 0.5 Million People." *BMC Medical* 20, no. 1 (2022): 134–147. https://doi.org/10.1186/s12916-022-02330-3.

Dairy and Prostate Cancer:
Orlich, M. J., A. D. Mashchak, K. Jaceldo-Siegl, et al. "Dairy Foods, Calcium Intakes, and Risk of Incident Prostate Cancer in Adventist Health Study–2." *American Journal of Clinical Nutrition* (June 8, 2022). https://doi.org/10.1093/ajcn/nqac093.

Lu, W., H. Chen, Y. Niu et al. "Dairy Products Intake and Cancer Mortality Risk: A Meta-analysis of 11 Population-Based Cohort Studies." *Nutritional Journal* 15, no. 1 (2016): 91. https://doi.org/10.1186/s12937-016-0210-9.

Dairy and Lung, Breast, and Ovarian Cancer:
Ji, J., J. Sundquist, and K. Sundquist. "Lactose Intolerance and Risk of Lung, Breast, and Ovarian Cancers: Aetiological Clues from a Population-Based Study in Sweden." *British Journal of Cancer* (October 14, 2014). https://pubmed.ncbi.nlm.nih.gov/25314053/.

Dairy and Water Use + Water Pollution:
https://www.sciencedirect.com/science/article/abs/pii/S2352801X21000977

Milk and Colic:
http://www.ncbi.nlm.nih.gov/pubmed/6823433

Cow's Milk Allergy Among Children:
https://www.ncbi.nlm.nih.gov/pmc/articles/PMC9046619/

43 Million Gallons of Milk Wasted:
https://www.wsj.com/articles/americas-dairy-farmers-dump-43-million-gallons-of-excess-milk-1476284353

Land Use for Livestock:
https://ourworldindata.org/global-land-for-agriculture

Dairy Cows and Antibiotics:
https://www.ncbi.nlm.nih.gov/pmc/articles/PMC7277698/

Estrogen in Dairy:
https://www.pcrm.org/news/news-releases/dairy-consumption-linked-prostate-ovarian-breast-cancers-finds-new-narrative

Livestock & GHG emissions study:
https://academic.oup.com/af/article/9/1/69/5173494

Cheese & Saturated Fat Consumption:
https://www.ncbi.nlm.nih.gov/pmc/articles/PMC3751311/

Dairy and Heart Disease:
Chen M, Li Y, Sun Q, et al. "Dairy Fat and Risk of Cardiovascular Disease in 3 Cohorts of US Adults." *American Journal Clinical Nutrition* (August 24, 2016). https://doi.org/10.3945/ajcn.116.134460.

Dairy and Air Quality, Emissions, and Public Health:
https://switch4good.org/the-impact-of-meat-and-dairy-production-on-air-quality

Dairy Consumption Associated with Acne:
https://jamanetwork.com/journals/jamadermatology/article-abstract/2767075

BOOKS

Barnard, Neal D. *The Cheese Trap*. New York: Balance, 2017.

Barnard, Neal D. *Your Body in Balance*. New York: Balance Books, 2020.

Briden, Lara. *Period Repair Manual*. Greenpeak Publishing, 2017.

Campbell, T. Colin, and Thomas M. Campbell II. *The China Study*. Dallas: BenBella, 2016.

Greger, Michael. *How Not to Die*. New York: Flatiron Books, 2015.

Hill, Simon. *The Proof Is in the Plants*. North Sydney, New South Wales: Penguin Life, 2021.

Animals are
Someone
not
Something

Index

Note: Page references in *italics* indicate photographs.

C

D

N

O

P

Q

R

S

T

V

Y

Z

About the Author

Bailey Ruskus, also known as Chef Bai, is a seasoned chef, activist, and holistic nutrition coach with an audience of nearly one million people. Classically trained at Le Cordon Bleu in San Francisco, she uses her culinary expertise to create rich flavors with clean, nourishing ingredients, and has been a professional chef for the past fourteen years in restaurants and privately around the world. She is an advocate for people with chronic health ailments, animal welfare, and the environment. Her own plant-based journey started with her desire to heal her chronic pain from a sixteen-year battle with endometriosis after exhausting all other options. She furthered her studies with a certification in plant-based nutrition from T. Colin Campbell Center for Nutrition Studies, and is a certified health coach from the Institute for Integrative Nutrition. Bailey now owns her business with her husband, Steve. They cook together for pop-up dinners; educate tens of thousands of people across the globe through their challenges, social media, and public speaking; develop recipes for their blog, magazines, and brands; consult with restaurants for a more sustainable future; and work one-on-one with individuals and families looking to heal through food. She is the author of the bestselling cookbook, *Cook. Heal. Go Vegan!* Bailey lives in sunny San Diego, California, with Steve, and their two rescue pups, Coconut and Piña.